Chip Carving
WORKSHOP

More Than 200 Ready-to-Use Designs

Lora S. Irish

FOX CHAPEL
PUBLISHING

© 2013 by Lora S. Irish and Fox Chapel Publishing Company, Inc., East Petersburg, PA.

Chip Carving Workshop is an original work, first published in 2013 by Fox Chapel Publishing Company, Inc. The patterns contained herein are copyrighted by the author. Readers may make copies of these patterns for personal use. The patterns themselves, however, are not to be duplicated for resale or distribution under any circumstances. Any such copying is a violation of copyright law.

ISBN 978-1-56523-776-6

Library of Congress Cataloging-in-Publication Data

Irish, Lora S.
  Chip carving workshop / Lora S. Irish.
      pages cm
  Includes index.
  ISBN 978-1-56523-776-6
  1. Wood-carving. 2. Wood-carving--Patterns. 3. Relief (Decorative arts) I. Title.
  TT199.7.I745 2013
  736'.4--dc23
                              2012046887

To learn more about the other great books from Fox Chapel Publishing, or to find a retailer near you, call toll-free 800-457-9112 or visit us at *www.FoxChapelPublishing.com*.

Note to Authors: We are always looking for talented authors to write new books. Please send a brief letter describing your idea to Acquisition Editor, 1970 Broad Street, East Petersburg, PA 17520.

Printed in China
First printing

ABOUT THE AUTHOR

My first memories of wood carving date back to when I was about ten years old. That fall, my father set up a small, low workbench in the red room and brought out a stack of long pine boards. He clamped one of the boards to the workbench and began drawing lines on it with his ruler and pencil. Then, with an odd-shaped knife that I now know was a large chip carving stab knife, he began cutting and shaving the wood between the lines. Over several days' time, big, beautiful stars began to appear on the board.

When one board had a complete line of stars, he would put it away and bring out a new board to work. Sometimes it would be very difficult for Dad to make the cuts as my brothers and I would be sitting so close to see what he was doing that he simply couldn't move his arms. And I remember Mom helping him put bandages on the blisters where he held the knife.

One evening, the long boards were gone and a new large, wide board appeared. This time, Dad carefully traced a design to the center of the board. We all watched as he made long, deep, curved cuts along the design lines. Magically two wondrous ruffled-neck, long-tailed, fighting roosters appeared—all made out of triangles. In a few more days' work, those roosters were joined by the same big stars.

When the rooster board was done everything disappeared—the long star boards, the rooster board,

Lora S. Irish

and the workbench; all of the knives were put away, and the wood chips were swept up.

Christmas morning that year, I discovered what happened to those star boards. There under the Christmas tree was a golden yellow pine Hope Chest decorated with chip carved stars and two fighting roosters and with a big red ribbon and tag: "To Susie, Love Dad." I cried with joy.

My Rooster Hope Chest is still my most precious possession and sits proudly on my dresser. Perhaps that was the beginning of my love of woodcarving and chip carving.

About Classic Chip Carving Grids

The wood art of chip carving dates back to A.D. 300 to 900 during the Migration Period of the Germanic people. Few wood samples have survived, but early chip carving can be seen throughout Europe and the British Isles in metalwork, created through the process of casting.

Today chip carving, also called spoon carving, uses both geometric cut shapes and free-form designs to create intricate and detailed patterns. The chips—small triangles, squares, or free-form curves—are cut into the flat surface of the wood using a chip knife or detail knife, and a chip carving stab knife.

Hope chests, carved wooden spoons, jewelry chests, clocks, candle plates, serving trivets, and decorative plaques are just a few ideas for your chip carving craft.

In this book, you will learn about chip carving tools, knife sharpening techniques, and wood preparation. The practice project will guide you through the steps to cut the three basic chip carving shapes: the classic chip triangle, the straight-walled triangle, and free-form lines.

The designs throughout this book are worked as gridded patterns that allow you to create your own unique chip carvings. To assist you in working your designs, traditional layouts are explored, and you will find a multitude of complete chip patterns in square, rectangular, oval, circular, and border designs. As an extra aid in mastering chip carving grids, there are blank graphs at the back of the book that can be traced or scanned for pattern creation.

Contents

Large Candle Plate
See pattern on page 92.

CHAPTER 1

Basic Chip Carving Techniques

There are many styles of woodcarving: bas relief designs, three-dimensional caricature carving, wood spirit walking sticks, and realistic duck decoys…to name a few. Of all the styles, chip carving stands out as the most unique, with designs created using the geometric shapes of the triangle, square, and free-form lines. Perhaps it could be said that chip carving is to woodcarving as quilt squares are to sewing.

The craft of chip carving requires just a few tools: a good knife, a smooth board, a pencil, a ruler, and a little recreational time. As you read through this section, you will learn about the basic steps and techniques used in chip carving. We will explore knife selection, knife sharpening, how to prepare your wood blank, and how to transfer your pattern to your board.

Next, we will work through the basic steps to make a clean, smooth chip each time, including basic hand positions, knife positions, gang cutting, and what to do if you have a chip out.

PREPARATION

The first step in any carving session is to gather your tools, wood, and crafting supplies. The chip carving knives and sharpening stones are available through any woodcarving supply store. Basswood carving blanks, acrylic craft paints, and graphite paper can be picked up at large craft stores or through online art supply stores. As you collect the tools and supplies you will be using, you may wish to create a kit or tote specifically for your chip carving.

Gather your tools and materials before you begin.

Wood

Many woods can be used for chip carving, including sugar pine, white pine, mahogany, soft maple, butternut, and basswood.

Basswood is easy to carve, with tight, clean, white grain lines, and it is available in pre-routed shapes: plates, plaques, and jewelry boxes. The finished samples throughout this book are worked in basswood.

No matter which wood species you chose, begin any chip carving session by smoothing the working surface with fine, 220-grit sandpaper. Work the sanding strokes with the direction of the wood grain. Remove the sanding dust with a dry tack cloth.

Always sand the wood before you start—even if you have decided to use a precut plaque.

Patterns

Grid motif layouts can be transferred to your wood using several methods.

1. Use a ruler and a 4H pencil to mark the grid lines directly on the wood surface. Use a 2B pencil to mark the chip triangles on the grid. This method creates a pale-lined grid with a darkly lined layout pattern.

2. Make a copy of the grid and layout on a sheet of paper that fits the shape of your board. Position the layout on the board, tape the edges to secure it, and then slide a sheet of graphite paper under the layout. Trace along the chip pattern lines.

3. Create a copy of the pattern on a sheet of paper that fits the shape of your board. Using rubber cement, coat both the wood surface and the back of the pattern following the manufacturer's directions. Press the layout paper in place on the wood. The glued paper will remain in place as you work the knife cuts through the paper into the wood. When the chip carving is complete, remove the remaining paper pattern pieces.

Carbon paper placed face down between the pattern and the wood is one of several transfer methods.

Tips

Use these basic organization techniques and a proper hand position to help make consistent cuts.

Mark the chips. Make a small pencil or marker dot on the board to note which chips to cut. The mark will be removed when the chip is made.

Hand position one. Hold the chip carving knife with the handle diagonally across the fold of the palm. This grip position is natural and very comfortable.

Rest the side of the hand lightly on the wood with the thumb extended to balance the hand. The knife blade meets the wood at an angle that creates the angle of the chip walls. A low angle to the blade creates shallow chips; a steep angle creates deep chips.

Make a cutting stroke by moving the entire arm, not just the fingers or hand.

Cut small chips by placing the point of the knife at the corner of the chip. Push the point into the wood. Roll the knife blade down until the blade cuts the complete line, ending at the end of the chip line.

To cut long chips, use a push and then a pull stroke to bring the knife blade to the end of the line.

Hand position two. Flip the blade over in your hand to cut the second leg of a chip without having to reposition the wood plaque.

Gang cuts. Repeating motifs and borders can be gang cut. Simply cut the side of each chip triangle in multiple motifs or within the border at one time. Then, rotate the board and make all of the cuts for the second leg of the triangles. Rotate the board again to make the final cut of the triangles.

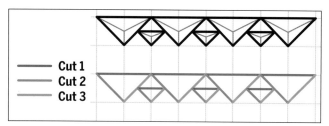

Gang cuts reduce board movement.

Chip outs. Chip outs happen because of an incorrectly angled cut, grain line problems, or extremely shallow cuts. Tear outs happen because of a dull blade edge. Both misfortunes can be repaired by gluing the chip to the board with a small dot of wood glue or super glue.

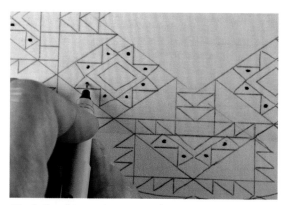

Mark the chips to be removed.

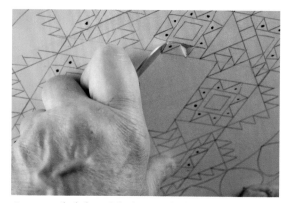

An extended thumb balances the hand.

Flip the blade to cut the other side.

Watch for chip outs and tear outs.

Sharpening

Of all the elements, supplies, and tools used in creating a chip carving, the angle and quality of your knife blade edge are perhaps the most important influences in cutting the clean sides of your chips. Chip carving knives are straight-edged, short-bladed tools that fit snuggly into the palm of your hand. The cutting edge of the chip knife needs to be sharpened to a low, long bevel that thins the blade as it approaches the cutting edge. Once the low bevel is created using the coarse sharpening stone, the knife is worked over a fine grit stone to create a sharp cutting edge. Working the knife edge over first your leather strop and then newspaper polishes the blade to a perfect cutting edge.

MATERIALS LIST

- Coarse ceramic stone, 1000- to 2000-grit, to create the bevel of the cutting edge
- Fine ceramic stone, 6000- to 8000-grit, to sharpen the cutting edge
- Emery cloth
- Leather strop
- Honing compound (I use red oxide rouge)
- Heavily printed newspaper

1 **Sharpen the blade.** When working either stone, lay your knife low against the stone's surface, pull the knife's edge across the stone, lift, turn, and then pull the opposite side of the knife across the stone.

2 **Strop the blade.** Strops have two sides: a finished leather side and a rawhide side. Coat the finished side with honing compound. Holding the knife low to the strop, pull the blade across the honing compound. Complete the stropping by working the blade over the raw leather side. Note: To keep your edge fresh, strop the blade often during any carving session. A few pulls across the strop every half hour ensures the sharpest edge possible.

3 **Polish the blade.** Give a final polishing to your blade by working it across a heavily printed newspaper page.

4 **Compare.** The upper left knife has been properly sharpened with a long, low bevel and is ready for chip carving. The lower right chip knife shows the factory honed edge.

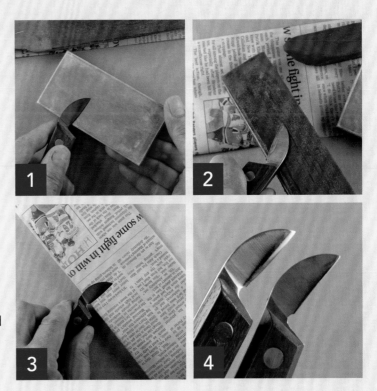

Practice Project

Heart border trivet

The greatest wonder of chip carving comes from the intricate geometric designs that can be created by learning how to cut three simple shapes: the triangle, the square, and the free-form line. Any of these three basic shapes can be altered by making them larger, smaller, longer, or taller, or by changing the angle of the element to the rest of the design.

As you work through this practice board, you will learn how to cut all three shapes, as well as how to create the straight wall chip cut. The focus in this section is on how to cut each style of shape. As you master the simple shapes in the practice board, you will be ready to cut any grid pattern presented in this book.

As a woodcarver, I work a practice board before any carving project I attempt. The practice board can be something as simple as a scrap of wood from the same species that I plan to use for the final carving. As I begin each new step or cut, I can go to the practice board and work the cut several times before I move to my primary project. The idea is that I get the motion and the amount of pressure down pat before I start to carve on my "good" board. The common mistakes photo at the end of this section is actually from one of my practice board sessions.

MATERIALS LIST

Cutting Tools

- Large chip carving knife
- Small chip carving knife
- Chip carving stab knife

Sharpening Tools

- Coarse ceramic stone, 1,000-grit
- Fine ceramic stone, 6,000-grit
- Leather strop
- Stropping compound or rouge
- Newspaper

Measuring Tools

- 4H pencil
- Ink pen
- Ruler
- Compass
- White artist's eraser

Wood Supplies

- Basswood blanks

Other Supplies

- Sandpaper, 220- to 320-grit
- Graphite paper
- Removable spray adhesive
- Acrylic craft paints
- Sanding sealer
- Polyurethane spray sealer
- Paper towels
- Assorted paintbrushes
- Large synthetic sponge

Built on a ¼" x ⅜" (5 x 10mm) grid.

Enlarge pattern 140% to fit Walnut Hollow 12" x 9" (305 x 230mm) oval plaque, #1839.

Cutting triangles

The classic chip triangle uses three cuts to create the incised shape.

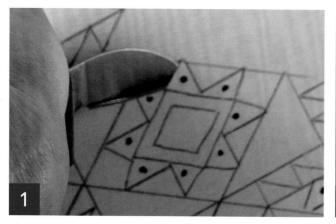

1

Make the first cut. Place the point of the blade in one end of one side of a triangle. Push the knife blade into the wood until the blade is sunk into the wood deep enough so that it reaches the opposite end of the line.

2

Make the second cut. Rotate the board to cut the second line of the chip in the same manner as the first. Begin this cut by pushing the knife point in the wood at the end of the first cut.

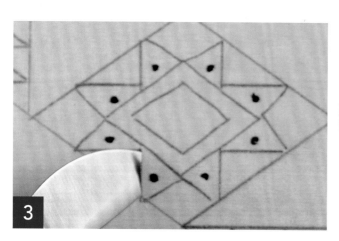

3

Make the third cut. Rotate the board again to make the third cut. This cut frees the chip.

Rotating vs. changing direction

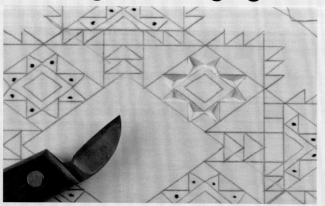

Whether you choose to make the triangle cuts by rotating the board or changing the direction of the knife in your hand is a personal preference for each chip carver.

My preference is to gang cut the triangles of a motif while rotating the board. For me, this sequence ensures that I maintain the same cutting blade angle throughout the entire chip work. Yet I do use both techniques in any carving.

Gang cutting the chips and rotating the board, not the knife direction, gives me the most consistent chip wall angles.

Adjacent triangles. *When possible, work the first cut of a new chip along the edge of the adjacent, previously cut chip.*

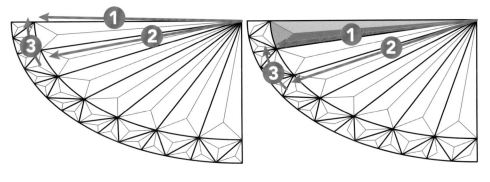

Long, narrow triangles and circle triangles. *For long triangle chips, especially those along a tight circular radius, work the first two cuts from the circle center point of the chip out toward the outer edge of the circular area. Complete the chip with the third cut along the outside, narrow edge of the triangle.*

Square and rectangle cuts

Square, rectangular, and trapezoid chips are made up of four or more cuts. As with triangle cuts, the work can be gang cut according to your preferences.

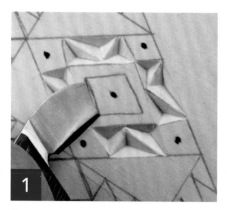

Start the cut. Place the point of the knife at one end of the chip's side line. Push the point toward the center of the square.

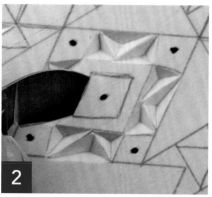

Make the remaining cuts. Rotate the board for each new side line cut.

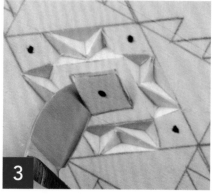

Free the chip. The chip is freed with the last, fourth cut.

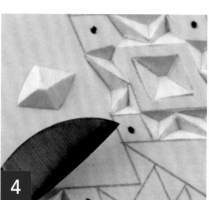

Check your work. A square chip should have consistent angles for each side with a center point—an inverted pyramid.

The center chip of this centerpiece motif is a square—four-sided—chip cut.

Straight wall chip cuts

Straight wall chip cuts are used inside a larger cut to create a terraced effect.

Start the cut. Make the two sides of the straight wall chip by holding the knife blade at a 90° angle to the wood surface. These cuts are deepest at the intersection point and taper back to the wood surface at the ends.

Make crisp corners. To ensure a crisply cut corner, you can recut these two sides from the taper to the deep point, rolling the tip of the blade into an upright position at the intersection.

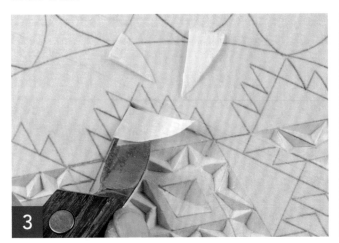

Slice deep. The third cut of the straight wall chip is made by laying the side of the knife low to the wood and then slicing into the deep corner.

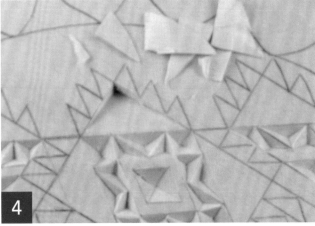

Taper the third side. The completed third side tapers from the height of the wood surface into the deep corner area of the chip.

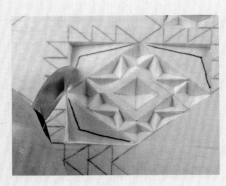

Note the terraced effect created by the smaller, straight wall cut inside a larger cut.

The slanted third cut of the smaller straight wall chip will have a steeper angle than the large chip.

Borders

Chip carved borders create a unique edge around a carving. The border can either use elements from the center motif or provide a pleasing contrast to it. Consider a geometric chip carved border or a free from chip carved border.

Heart border

The sides of any chip can be curved, as in this heart border example. The curved triangles of the heart border accent the oval shape of the plaque.

Start the cut. To cut a curved side chip for the heart border, place the point of the knife at one end of the line. Push the tip into the wood to establish the depth of the corner.

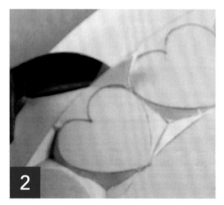

Follow the line. Pull the knife from the corner following the curve of the line.

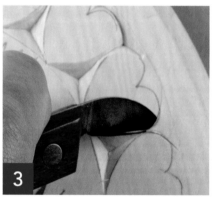

Concentrate on the arc. Curved chips can be either convex or concave arcs.

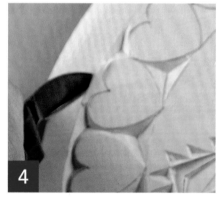

Make the curved cuts. Surround the heart with curved triangle chips.

Add accents. Use a stab knife to make small accent cuts inside the heart. Simply push the point of the knife into the wood to create the tight triangle cut.

Sawtooth border

The sawtooth border is a motif that is often used to surround a square motif. It can also be used as a stand-alone border accent.

The sawtooth motif is worked as any other classic triangle chip shape and is easy to gang cut.

The complex look of this centerpiece motif is created by working one chip shape at a time: the classic triangle, the square, the straight wall, and sawtooth border.

Free-form chip carving

Free-form chip cuts are made using two cuts along a flowing curved line. You can vary any free-form line by changing the angle of the cuts and the distance between the two cuts—a thick-thin-thick effect.

Trace the pattern. Begin this step by tracing the small free-form heart pattern (see page 11) to the center of the layout using graphite paper.

Start the cut. Place the point of the knife at one end of the free-form line. Using the same angle as any classic triangle chip, pull the knife along the line, slowly deepening the cut as you near the center point of the line. Begin to raise the blade tip as you continue to the other end of the free-form line. Then, rotate the board to make a second cut along the free-form line in the same manner.

Spoon carving

One specific type of free-from chip carving is called spoon carving. This chip has two arched sides to create a spear point shape. Spoon chip motifs are often found on Victorian clock shelves and on decorated rolling pins.

Start the cut. Place the point of the knife at the end of one line. Pull the knife point along the line, following the curve of the spoon shape.

Repeat the cut. Rotate the board and repeat the process for the second side of the spoon chip.

Common mistakes

Let's take a moment and look at a few common mistakes that can occur in any chip carving project.

The sample piece is a basswood practice board: ¼" (5mm) thick, 4" (100mm) wide, and 24" (610mm) long. As a habit, I will work a sampling of the motifs that I will be using in any layout on a practice board before I begin working on the full layout. This extra effort lets me experiment with each motif, practice the best way to make the cuts, and determine where I might have difficult-to-cut areas.

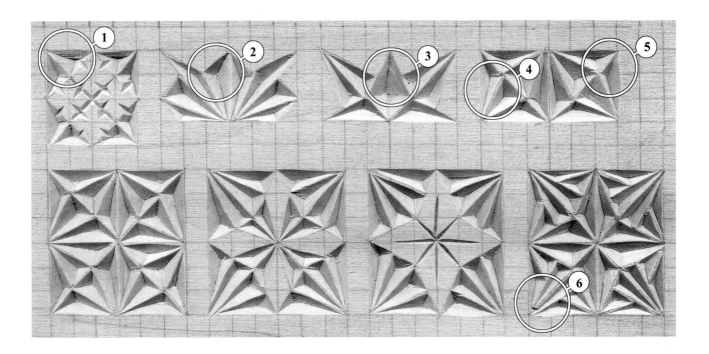

1. A rough, ragged wall on a chip cut, like the one shown here, is most often caused by an improperly sharpened knife. Your blade may be dented or dull, or it may be a blade with a beveled cutting angle that is too wide. Solution: Sharpen and/or reshape your blade.

2. The center intersection where several cuts meet should be crisp and clean. If a small portion of wood remains at the center intersection, then one of the side cuts was not made as deeply as the other cuts. Solution: Simply recut the shallow side to remove the excess wood.

3. The side wall of the chip should be smooth. This chip side was recut several times in small portions, which allows each newly cut line to show in the side wall. Solution: If you need to recut one side of a chip, cut the full side—not just a portion of that side.

4. Two adjacent chips should share a crisply edged line. The first cut of this second chip was made too far away from the first chip, leaving a wide, flat space of wood between the two chips. Solution: Recut the first side of the second chip to meet the adjacent chip triangle and create a crisp, sharp intersection.

5. As the long side of this chip was cut, the knife edge strayed from the straight line, causing a wobbled edge. Solution: Recut the entire side of this triangle to straighten the long wall.

6. Chip outs happen for two primary reasons. First and foremost is that the knife does not have a properly sharpened, low beveled cutting edge. The second reason comes from pulling the knife blade from the narrow point too quickly. Solution: Try pushing the tip into the narrow point slightly before you begin the pull portion of the cut. You can also pre-score extremely narrow chip triangle points by pulling the knife tip along the pattern line. Use no pressure and do not push into the wood—simply score the upper layer of fibers before you make the full cutting stroke.

Vintage painting

Basswood is an easy-to-carve wood, which makes it a wonderful surface for fine, tight chip carving. But it is also a very plain, white wood with no color changes or grain texture to add interest to the finished work. So I prefer to either stain or paint my finished chip carvings.

Because chip carving is an extremely old art style, a vintage painting technique is appropriate. The finished project will have the dark, aged, distressed look of a vintage chip carving.

MATERIALS LIST

- Sandpaper, 220-grit
- Clean, dry tack cloth
- Assorted stiff-bristle paintbrushes
- Tin foil, glass tile, or foam plate
- Paper towels
- Polyurethane or acrylic spray sealer
- Sea sponge or synthetic sponge

Acrylic Craft Colors

- Golden yellow
- Sienna brown
- Medium brown
- Red oxide or burnt sienna
- Dark or chocolate brown
- Black

1 **Prepare the surface.** Check your work for any clean-up cuts before you begin the painting steps. Lightly sand the surface as necessary with 220-grit sandpaper, and then remove any sanding dust with a clean, dry tack cloth.

2 **Mix paint colors.** On a tile or palette, place a medium amount of golden yellow and sienna brown acrylic craft color. Lightly mix the two colors where they touch on the tile, but do not totally mix them; allow some of each of the original colors to remain. If necessary, add a few drops of water to the colors to slightly thin the paint.

3 **Cover the surface.** With a large ox-hair brush, scrub one or two coats of this mix over the entire surface of the chip carving plaque. Vary the background color by making some brush strokes with one pure color or the other pure color, then add some brush strokes with the mixed color. Work any thick puddles of color out of the inside of the chip triangles. Allow the plaque to dry completely.

4 Apply the next coat. With a smaller flat-bristle brush, work one coat of red oxide on the uncarved areas of the centerpiece motif. Apply one coat of medium brown to the heart border and plaque edge. Allow the paint to dry. Note: These two colors do not need to be applied in a pristine manner as you will be distorting the edges of the painting in a coming step.

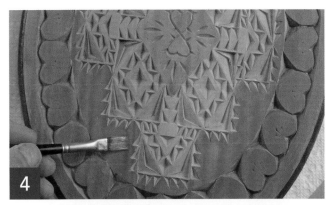

5 Mix brown and black. On your tile or palette, place a medium amount of dark chocolate brown and black acrylic craft color. Thin the paint slightly with water. Mix a small amount of the black with the brown so that you have three color tones on the tile or palette—chocolate, chocolate black, and black.

6 Apply brown and black. Work a small area at a time—about 3" to 4" (75–100mm) square. Using a flat-bristle brush, apply one coat of the brown and black antiquing colors to an area. Be sure that the inside cut areas of each chip are coated.

7 Continue applying color. Apply antiquing color to the plaque, varying the colors and wiping away the excess paint immediately with the sponge. When all areas have been worked, allow the paint to dry completely.

8 Sand the surface. Fold a large section of 220-grit sandpaper into quarters to create a stiff, flat sanding pad. Begin sanding the surface of the plaque to remove the paint along the chip triangle edges. Sand some areas lightly to remove just the antiquing color and some areas more vigorously to work back to the raw wood.

9 Remove any sanding dust. Use a soft brush of canned air to remove any dust left behind after sanding. Use several light coats of acrylic or polyurethane spray sealer, according to the manufacturer's directions, to finish the piece.

GALLERY

Sample Grid Wall Clock
See pattern on page 97.
This large wall clock uses multiple chip grids, making it a perfect sampler project. To create the aged wood look, coat the project with a base coat of light tan acrylic paint. Add white, ocher, and sienna acrylic streaks. After applying two coats of polyurethane sealer, the project can be antiqued using a medium or walnut brown oil stain. Add two more coats of polyurethane for the final finish.

Oval Kitchen Trivet

See pattern on page 99.
Free-form chip carving patterns are quick and easy. A few deep curved chip cuts make the center flower the main focus of this design. This trivet is finished in two light colors of brush-on polyurethane sealer.

Free-Form Leaf Plaque

See pattern on page 91.
You can combine free-form patterns with gridded chip motifs to create a new and unique design. To accent the chip work, two light coats of polyurethane sealer have been applied. The project was then antiqued with walnut brown oil stain. After the stain dried well, two more light coats of polyurethane were added.

Antique Wall Plate

See pattern on page 95. Triangle chips, straight wall chips, and free-form carving are combined in this candle plate pattern. Two coats of medium burnt sienna acrylic paint have been brushed onto the finished project. Next, two coats of polyurethane sealer were applied. The project was then antiqued using walnut brown oil stain. After the stain dried the inner ring of chips was heavily sanded. The project was finished with two more coats of polyurethane.

Small Heart Candle Plate

See pattern on page 93. To balance the deep free-from cuts in the center heart ring, the outer ring in the center of the plate uses large triangle chips. For this wall plate, the base acrylic coats were worked in forest green with an oil stain antiquing of black.

Fan Grid Candle Plate

See pattern on page 96. Even though the center motif uses tight, curved chip work to create the design, it is the uncarved central flower that becomes the focus. To keep this candle plate in the pale tones, seal the chip carving first with two coats of polyurethane sealer. Antique your chips using a medium green oil stain. Use two coats of polyurethane for the final finish.

Large Oval Kitchen Trivet

See pattern on page 94. The simple chip cut border of this trivet takes the design to the very edge of the wood. The soft Williamsburg look was created starting with a base coat of white acrylic paint. Two coats of polyurethane were added to protect the base color from the light blue oil stain. The project was finished with two more coats of polyurethane.

CHAPTER 2

Simple Layout Ideas

Because many of the classic chip carving motifs can be plotted on a square or rectangular grid, a huge variety of large layouts is possible. By starting with a specific layout, you can easily design an attractive and intricate piece that is well balanced.

On the following pages you'll find a number of simple layout ideas. Each can be used as a stand-alone pattern or combined with other motifs or borders.

Remember that the inclusion of blank space in a layout is also very important. A balance of empty and carved space can often place more emphasis on the carved areas by giving the viewer's eye a rest. Plan these blank spaces as carefully as you would a carved space.

A few common layouts included here are the Nine Patch, Sawtooth Border, Spacer, and Deck of Cards. Use the following guidelines for strong, bold layouts:

1. Use several different motifs to create a changing pattern of chip cuts. Two or three motifs laid out in a Nine-Patch design gives more impact than just one motif nine times.

2. Allow uncarved "air space" within the design. Chip cutting the entire surface of the wood can be overpowering for the viewer. Create air spaces within a motif by not cutting some chips and between motifs by adding a small spacer motif.

3. The final size of any motif is based on the size of each grid unit. For small motifs, use ¼" (5mm) or less squares for the grid layout; large motifs can be made using ½" (15mm) or larger grid squares.

4. You can plot any motif using a rectangular grid instead of a square grid. A grid rectangle that is ¼" (5mm) wide by ½" (15mm) high will create a motif that is twice as long as it is wide.

5. Border motifs are excellent for separating one area of your layout from another. Separate a centerpiece motif from a free-form design using a simple Sawtooth Border around the centerpiece.

6. Individual square motifs can be divided along either the horizontal or vertical lines to create new small triangular or rectangular designs.

7. Quilting magazines and online quilting sources can provide new ideas for chip carving layouts. Quilt square patterns may also provide ideas for both new motifs and new border patterns.

8. Record your layouts in a graph paper notebook. Once you have designed a layout, that layout can be changed by simply using different motif squares.

9. Inexpensive basswood boards, ¼" (5mm) thick by 18" (455mm) to 36" (915mm) long, can be purchased at many local hardware stores. They make wonderful practice boards on which you can try new motifs or layouts before you begin work on your basswood plaques.

10. Many traditionally angled triangle cut motifs can be worked as a straight wall cut. Do a practice sample to determine where the straight walls will fall in the final design.

11. Mixing traditional angled triangle cuts, straight wall cuts, and free-form chip carving makes a strong, dynamic finished layout.

12. A sample clock face can be incorporated into any layout. However it is not necessary to include all of the clock numbers in your final design. You may use all twelve numbers; just the compass point numbers of 12, 3, 6, and 9; a small star motif to represent the compass point numbers; and even no numbers at all.

WORKING WITH GRIDS

Grids allow more flexibility in chip carving. When
you work with grids, you are able to mix and match
elements as well as divide and reposition them.

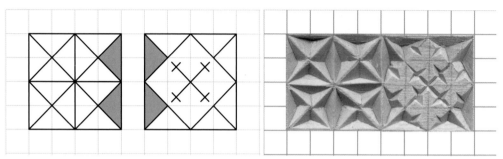

*When possible, match the side chips of adjacent motif squares. In the sample, both motifs use
two vertical triangle chips, which, when joined, lead the eye smoothly from one motif into
the next.*

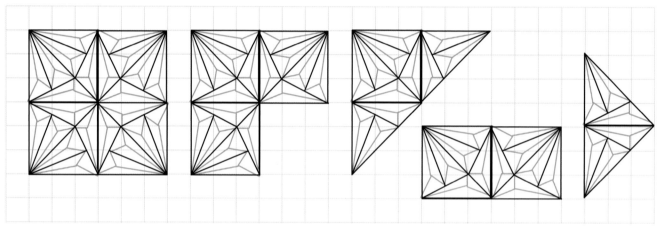

*Any square or rectangular motif can be divided into three-quarter, one-half, and one-quarter
sections, and those individual sections can be used to create the larger layout design.*

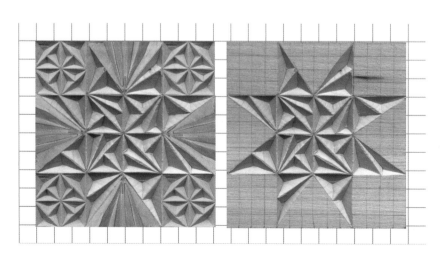

*Avoid overpowering your layout by
allowing uncarved air spaces between
areas within a motif or between motifs.
Because all of the space inside the square
is chipped in the left motif, the center
Flying Goose star, which is clearly seen in
the right hand sample, is not prominent.*

Nine Patch Layout

Work this simple layout in three rows of three grid patterns to create the Nine Patch square. This sample uses one grid for the center, one for the compass point positions, and one for each corner.

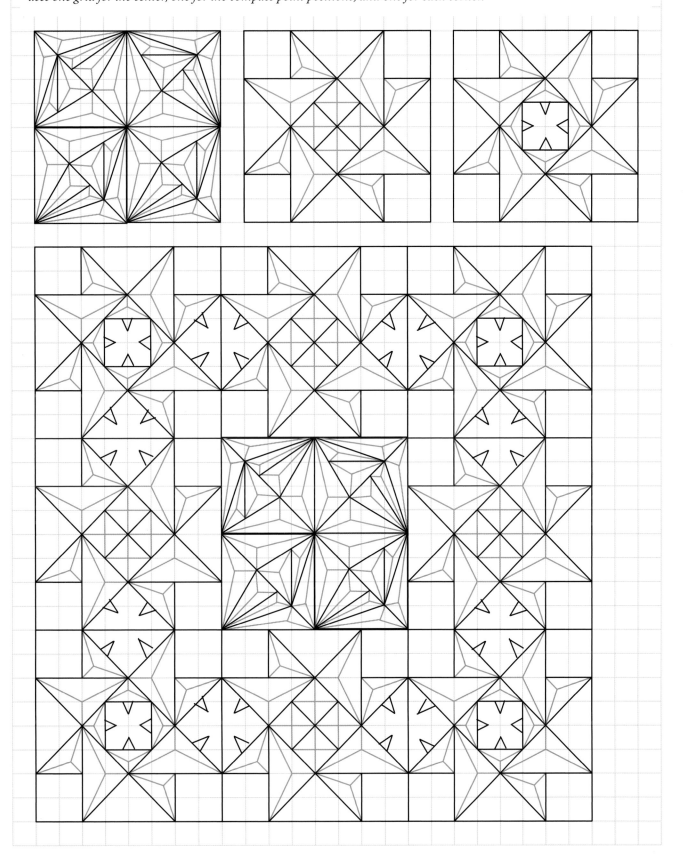

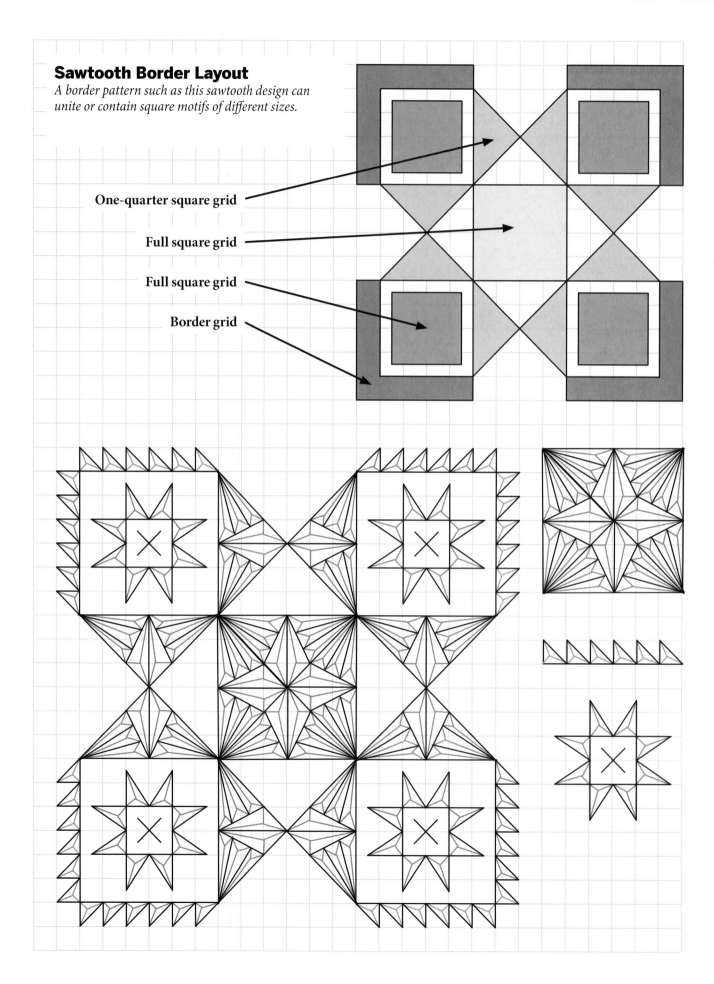

Sawtooth Border Layout

A border pattern such as this sawtooth design can unite or contain square motifs of different sizes.

One-quarter square grid

Full square grid

Full square grid

Border grid

Deck of Cards Layout

Deck of Cards layout uses three-quarter motifs that interlock at the center point of the design. This sample also features a border pattern the same width as the Deck of Cards' center with half-triangle motifs in each corner.

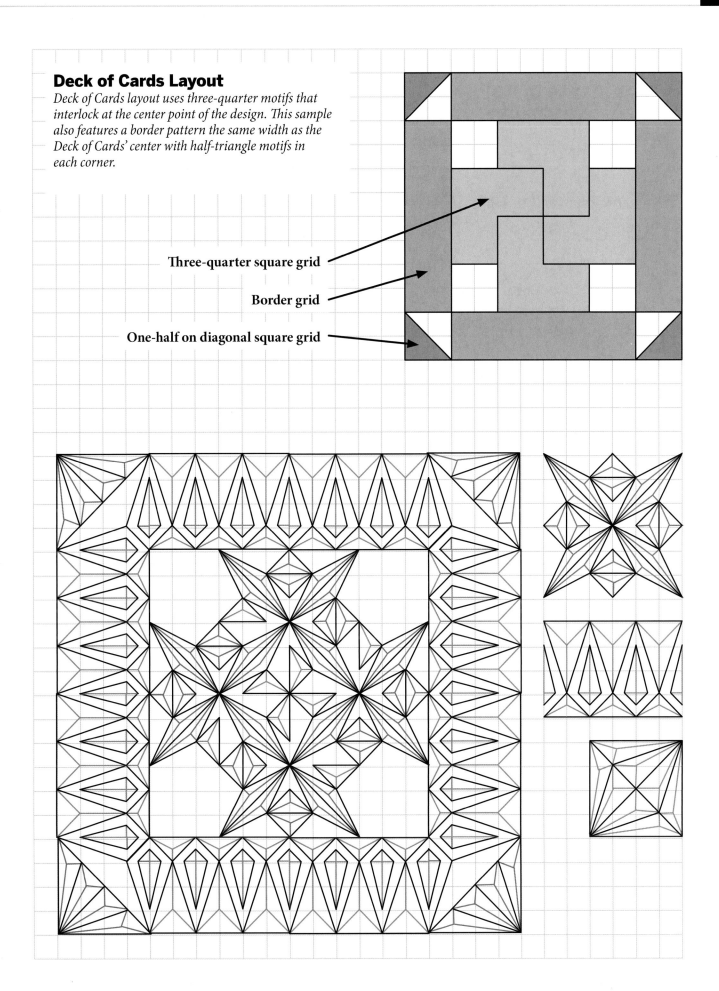

Three-quarter square grid

Border grid

One-half on diagonal square grid

Spacer Layout

Pattern motifs can be separated using small spacer motifs such as squares, small stars, or a complementary triangle shape that matches a side shape in the main motif.

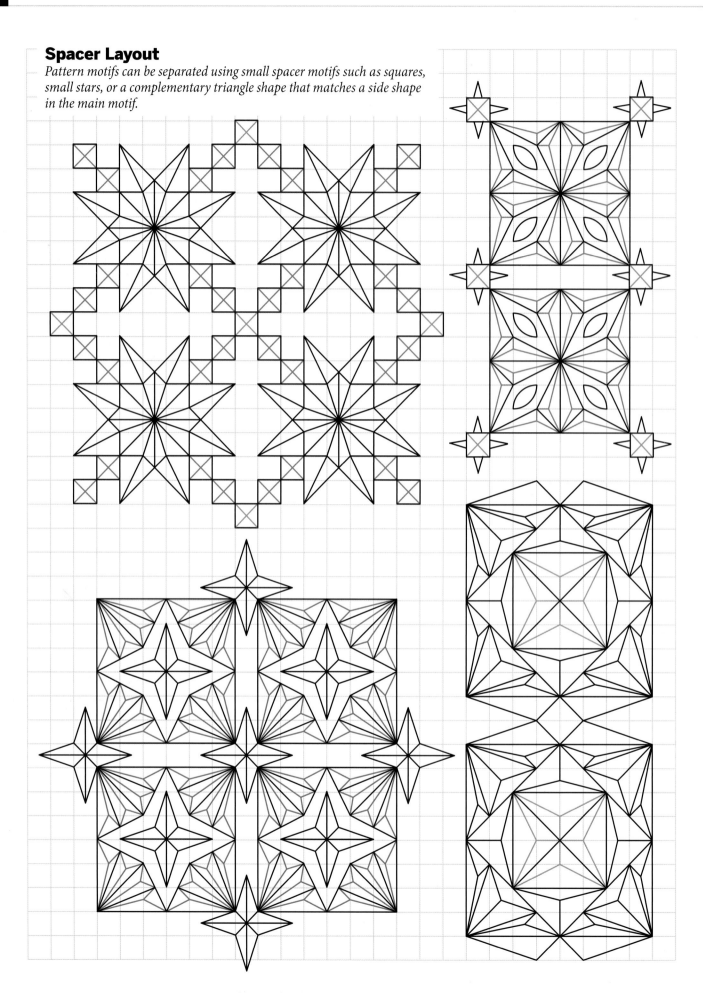

Corner Cropped Grid Layout

This corner cropped motif layout allows an open center space for a free-form monogram, date, or floral pattern.

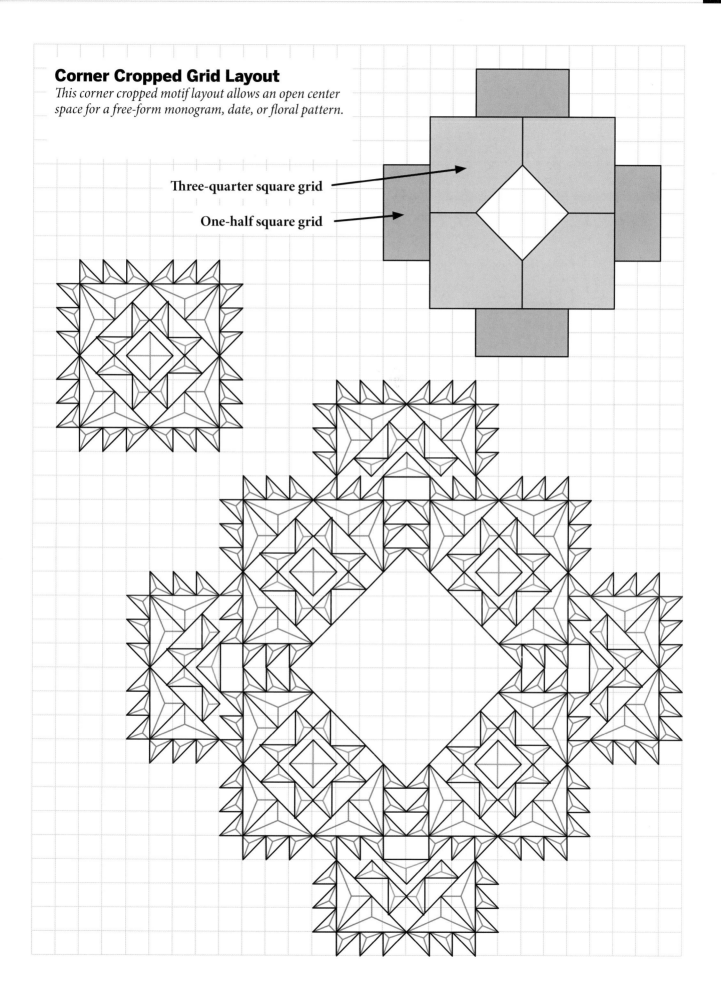

Three-quarter square grid

One-half square grid

Checkerboard Layout

Two square motifs make this layout. One is a large, intriguing motif that fills one square of the layout. The smaller motif is set in a Nine Patch design to create the second square. This layout is an excellent way to fill a large surface such as the top of a tack box or tabletop.

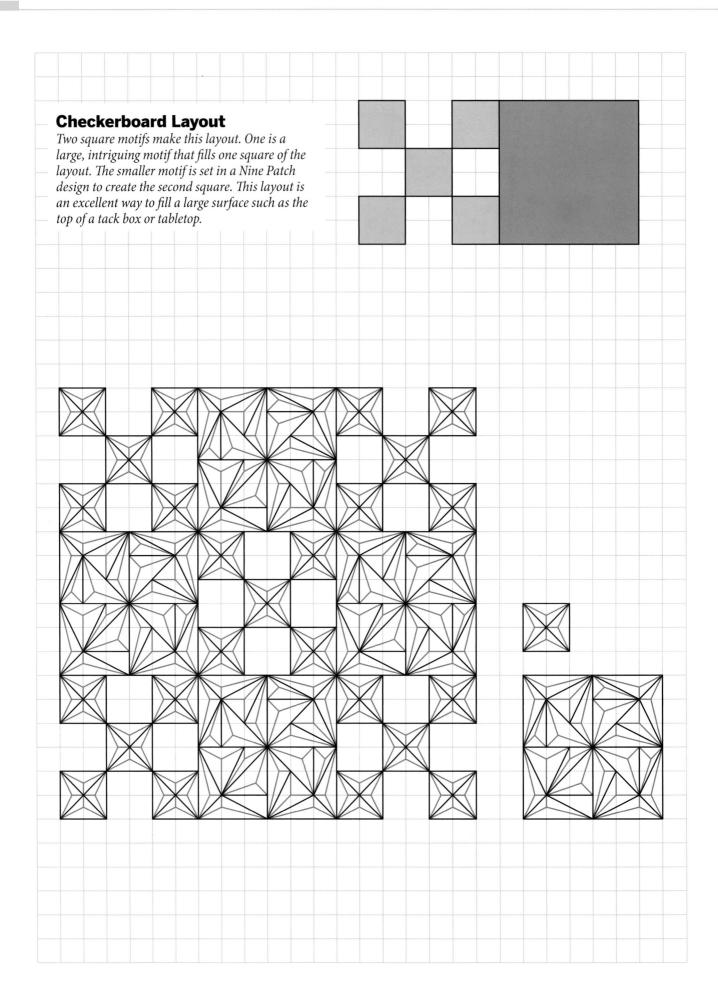

Tulip Layout

One large square motif and two half-triangle motifs make up the base of the tulip. A smaller square is then set in the angle of the half triangles to complete the flower look of this layout.

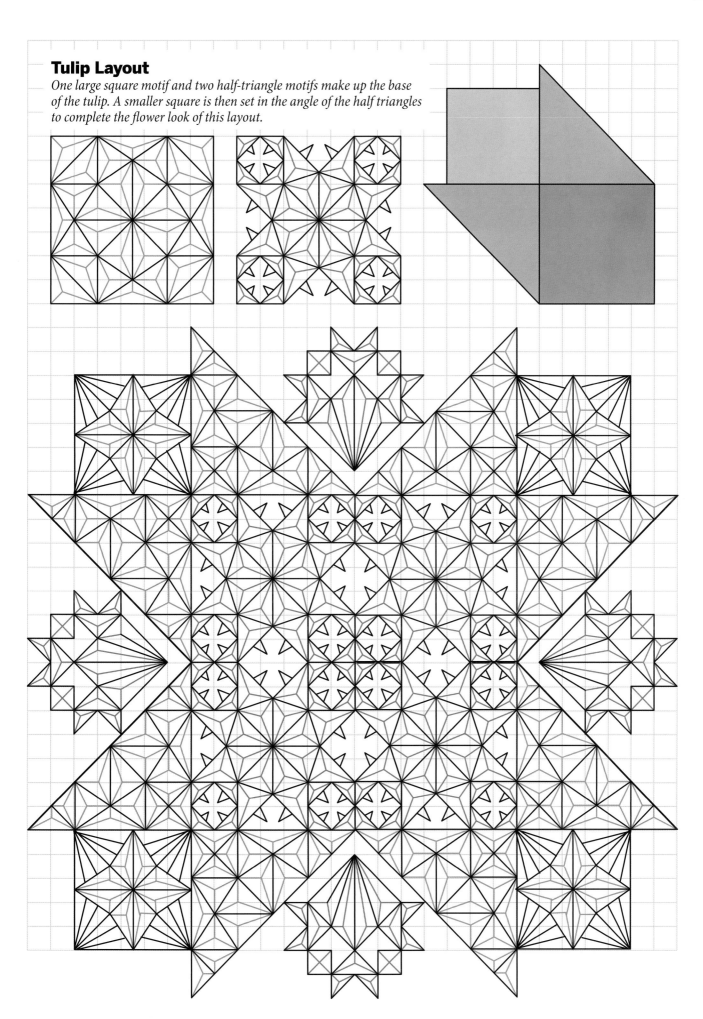

Cropped Nine Patch Layout

The open air space of this layout is increased by cropping the corner motifs.

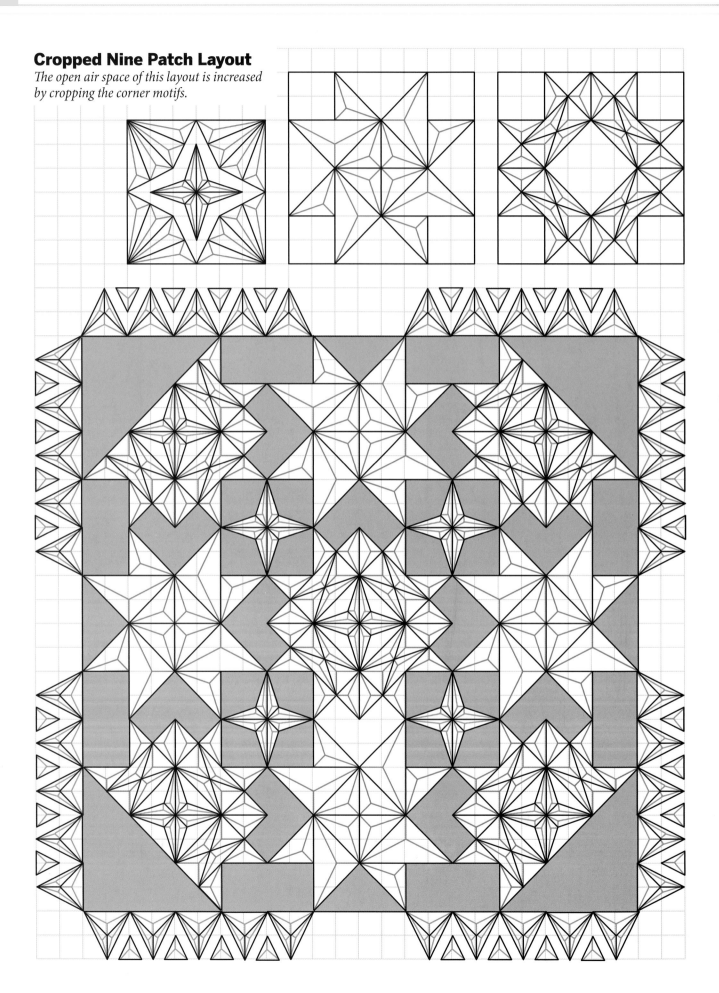

Double Wedding Rings Layout

This classic quilt pattern layout is made up of overlapping border pattern circles with a large cropped corner motif at each intersection. A smaller circle motif fills the inner circle areas.

CHAPTER 3

Chip Carving
Grids and Patterns

The chip carving motifs throughout this section are presented as gridded designs to make it easy for you to trace, replicate, and reproduce them in any size or combination of grid motifs.

For your convenience, they are sorted by the number of grid units needed to graph that pattern—a 4 x 4 grid motif is worked over a graph four units long by four units high. You can easily change the final size of any grid by changing the size of your graph unit. If you graph your 4 x 4 motif using ¼" (5mm) squares, your finished motif will measure 1" (25mm) square. By changing the graph unit to ½" (15mm) square your finished motif size will increase to 2" (50mm). Likewise, if you're working in centimeters, a 4 x 4 grid of 1cm square would give you a 4cm square motif.

To further increase your ability to create new sizes of motifs, you can make the graph units rectangles. A 4 x 4 grid motif can become a rectangle by making each unit ¼" (5mm) wide x ½" (15mm) high. The finished motif now measures 1" (25mm) wide x 2" (50mm) high. In a grid of centimeters, the same holds true: the height would be twice as long as the width.

Blank sample grids are presented in the back of this section for your convenience.

3 x 3 GRIDS

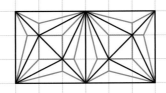
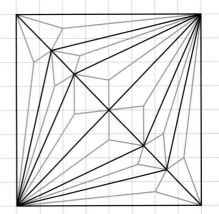

You will notice that once you have a basic pattern, you can adjust the shape or use elements of that original pattern to form many additional designs. All the designs on this page were derived from this original pattern.

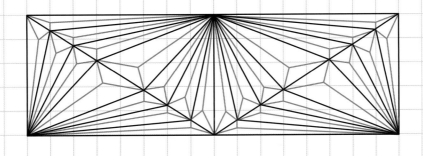

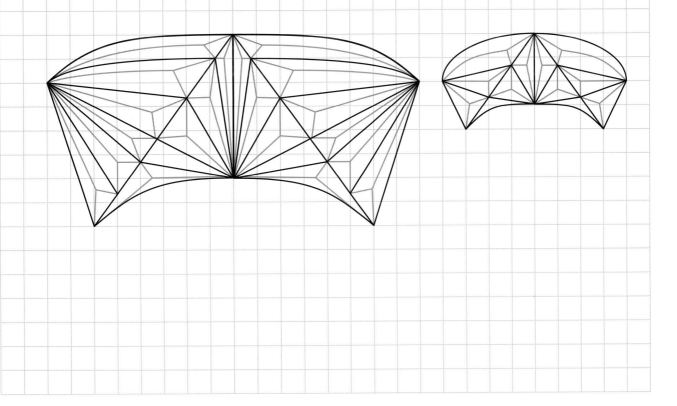

4 x 4 GRIDS

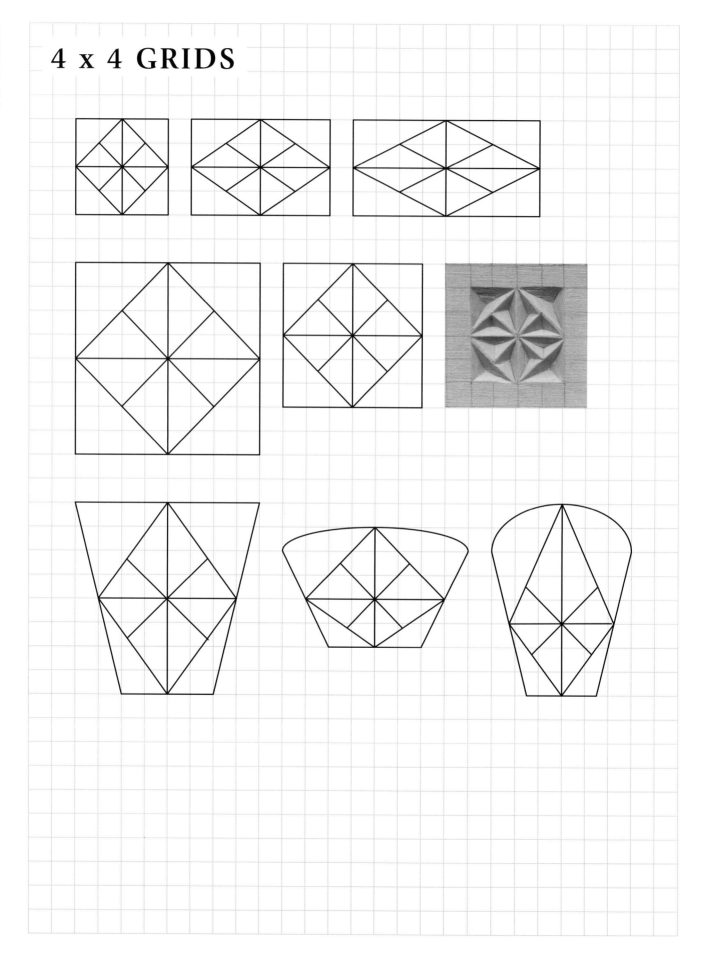

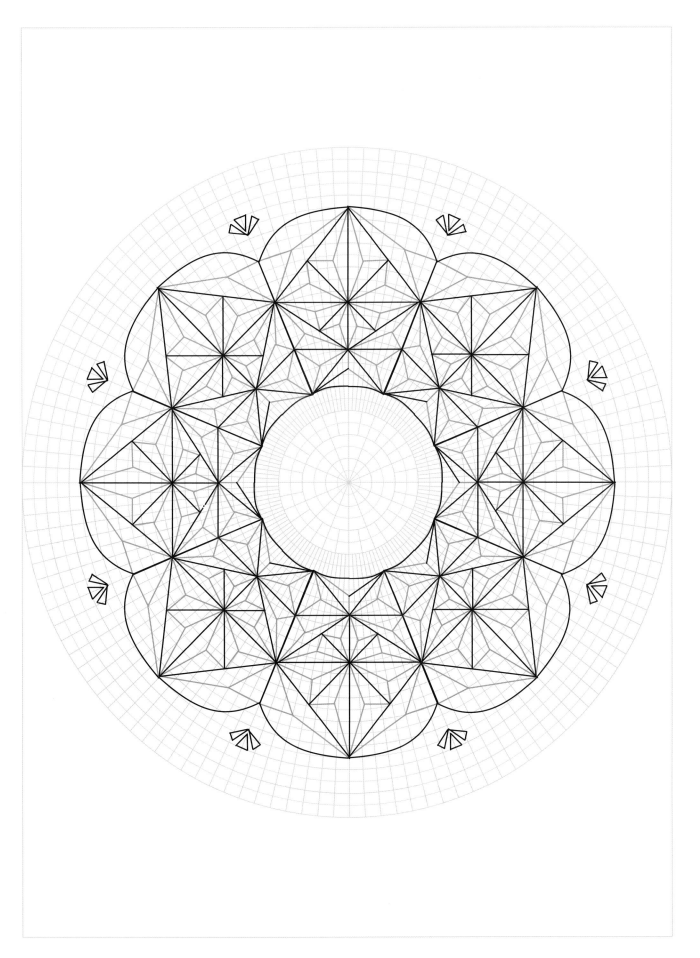

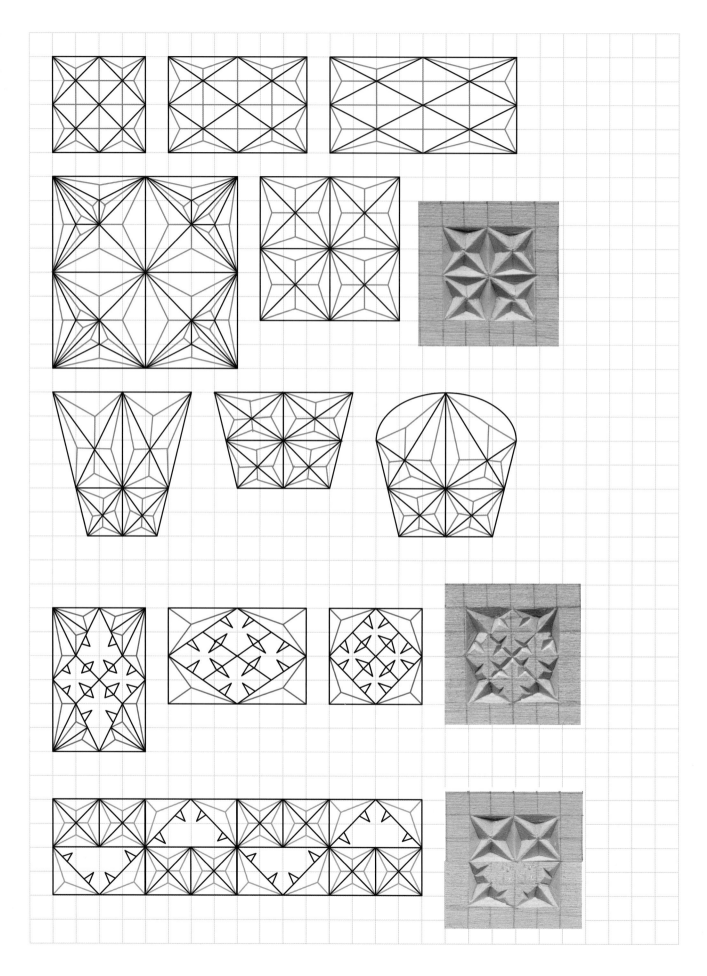

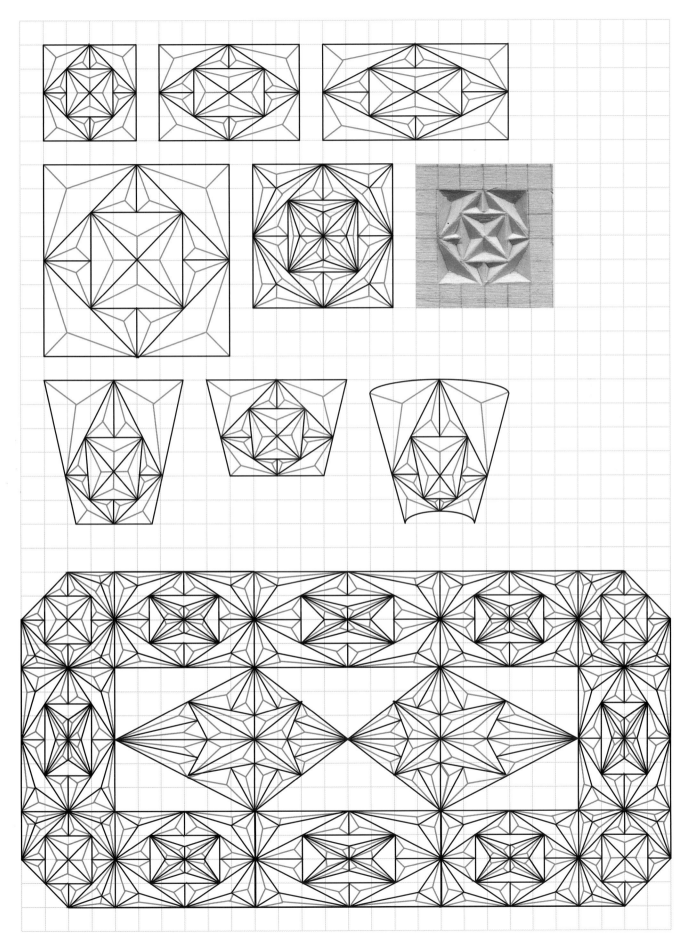

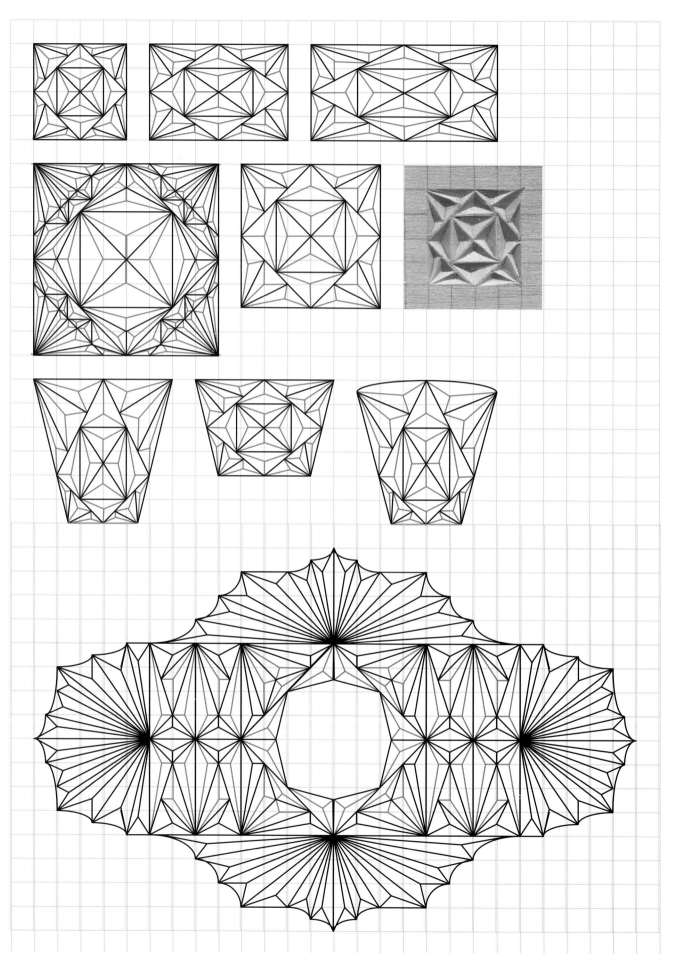

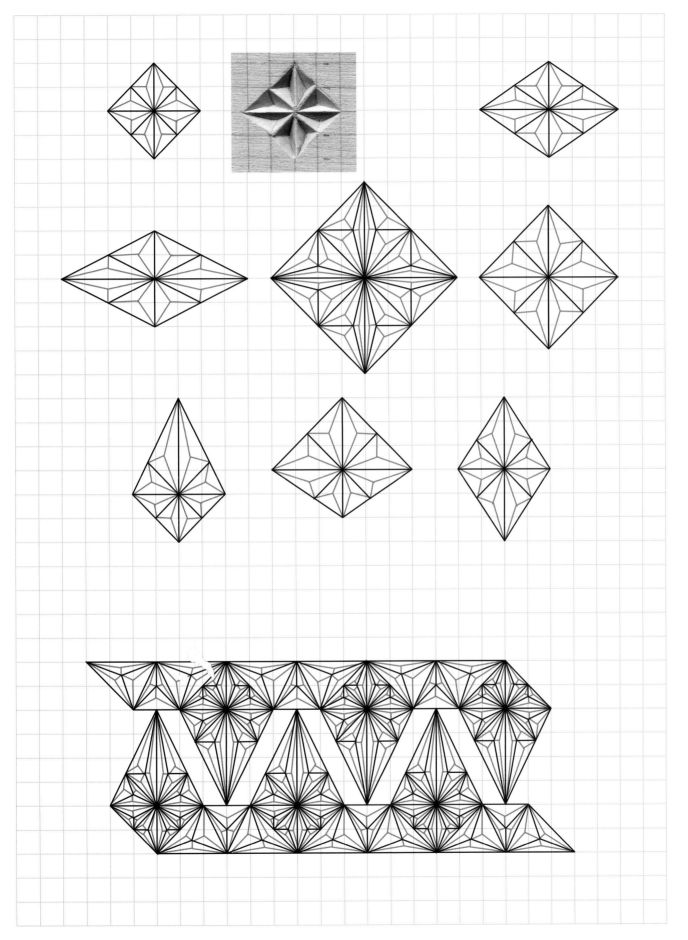

6 x 6 GRIDS

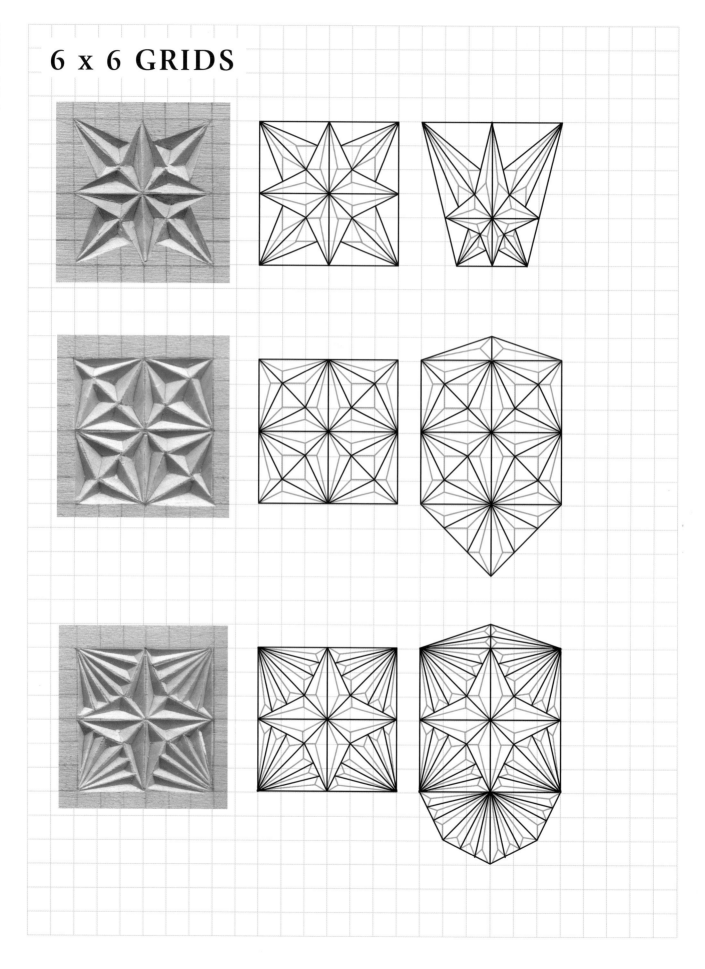

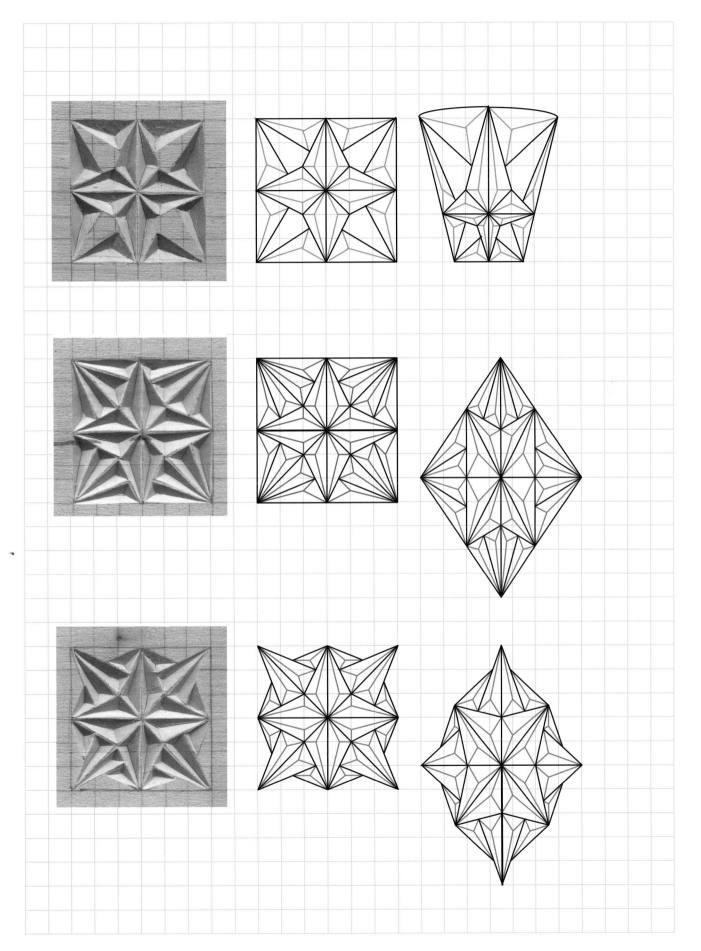

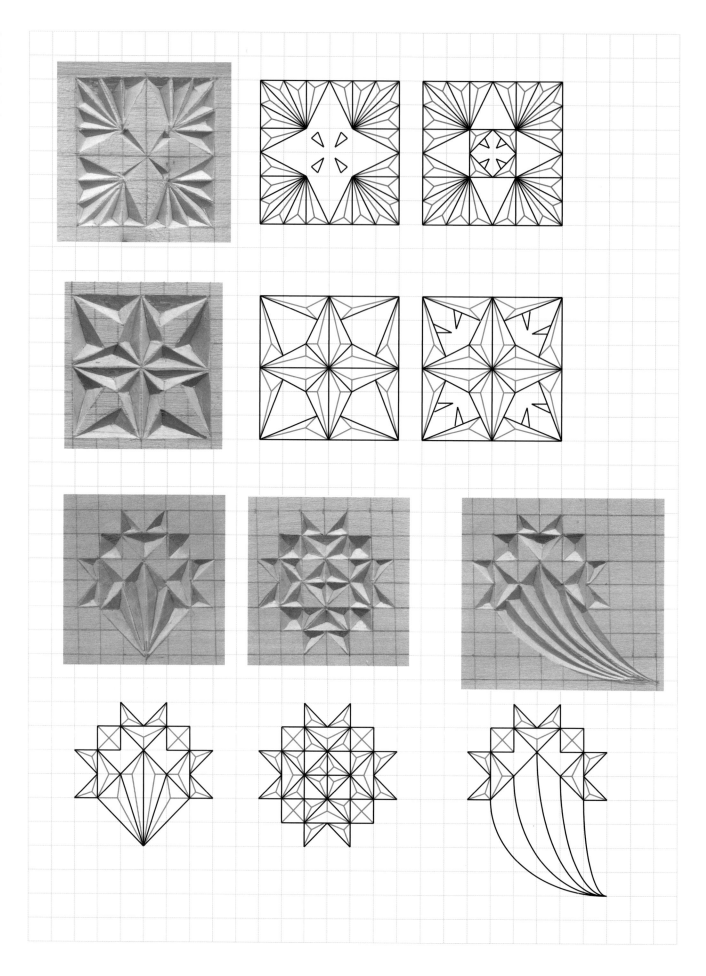

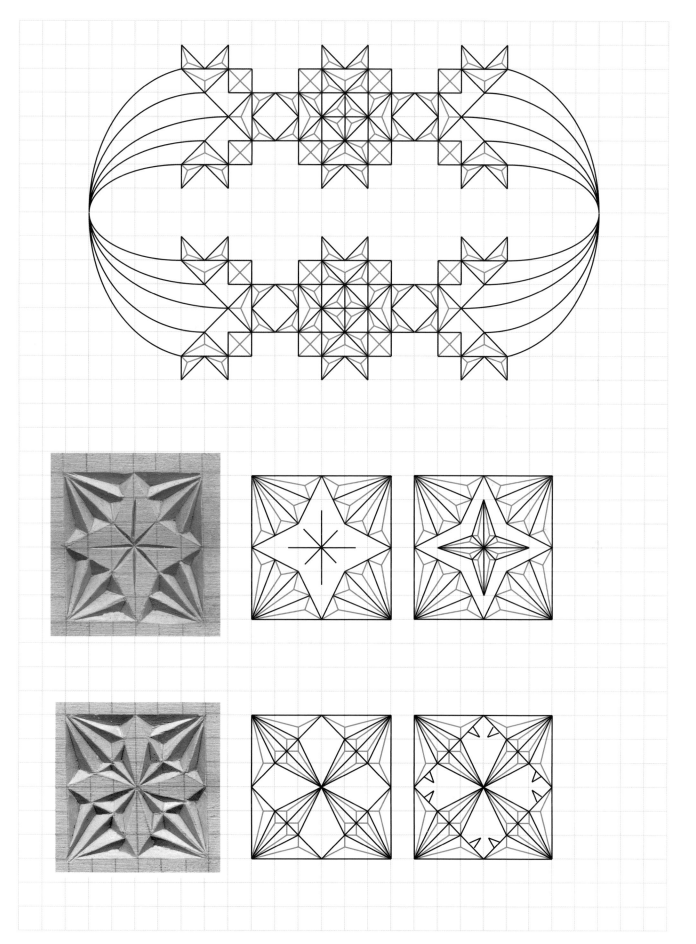

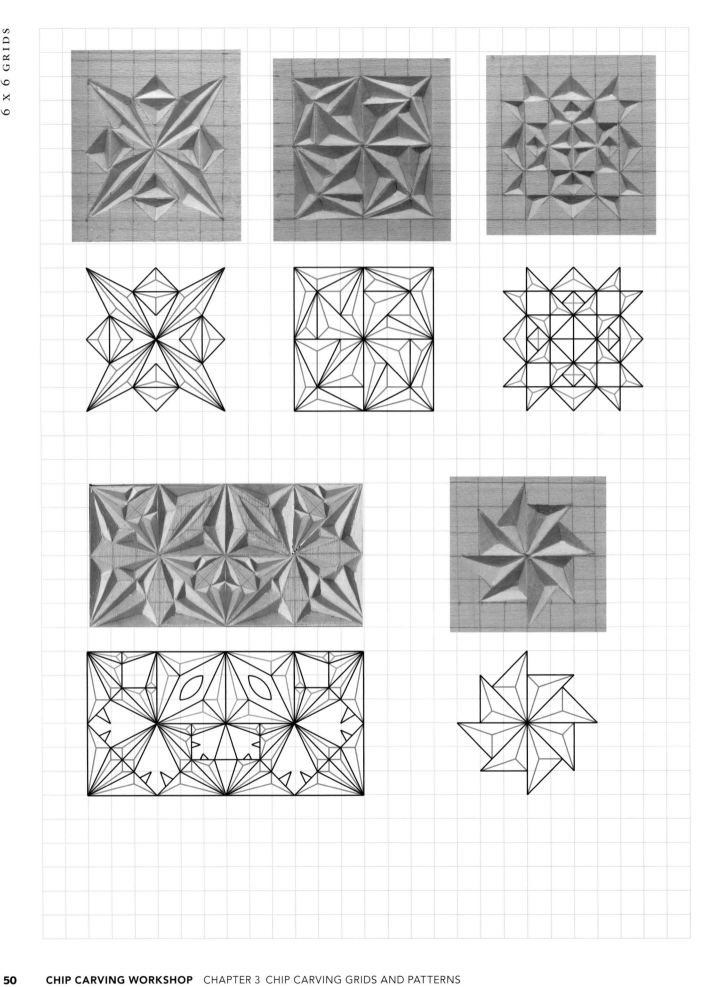

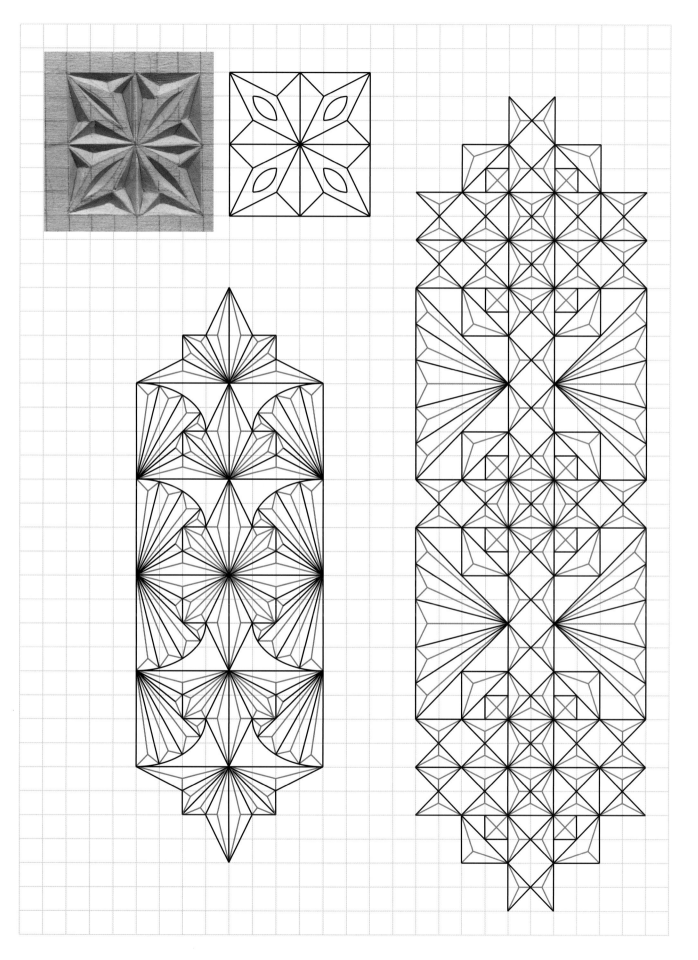

7 x 7 GRIDS

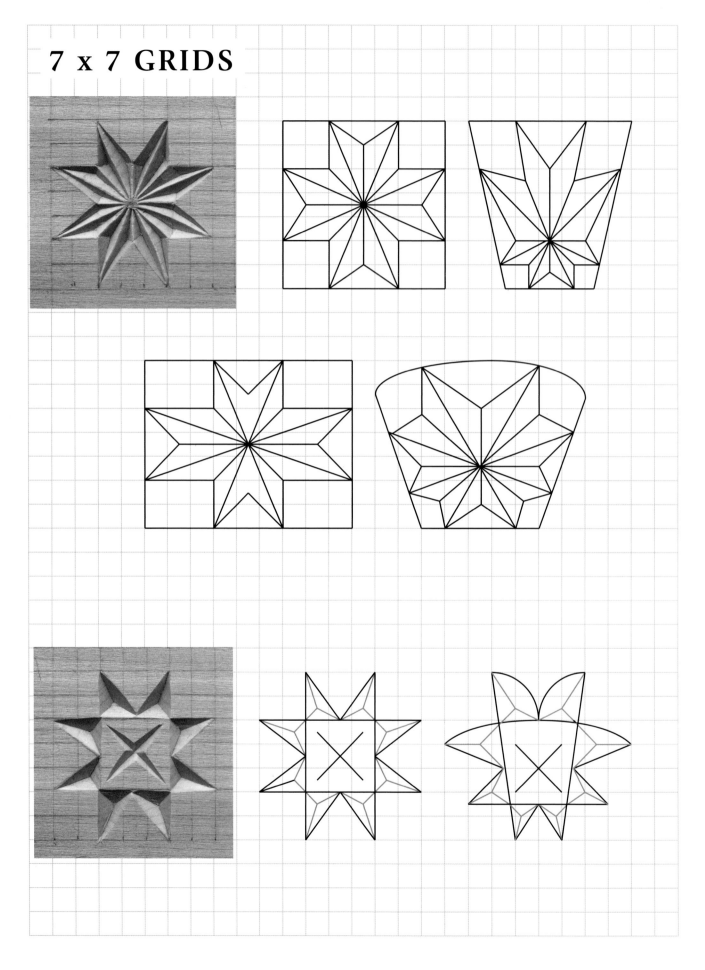

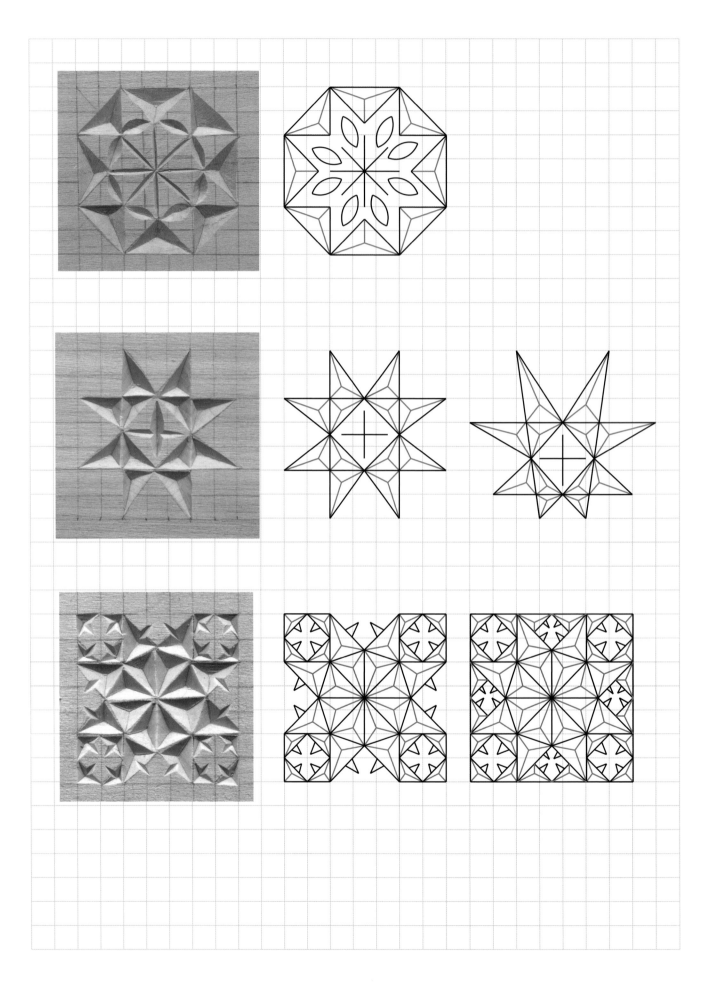

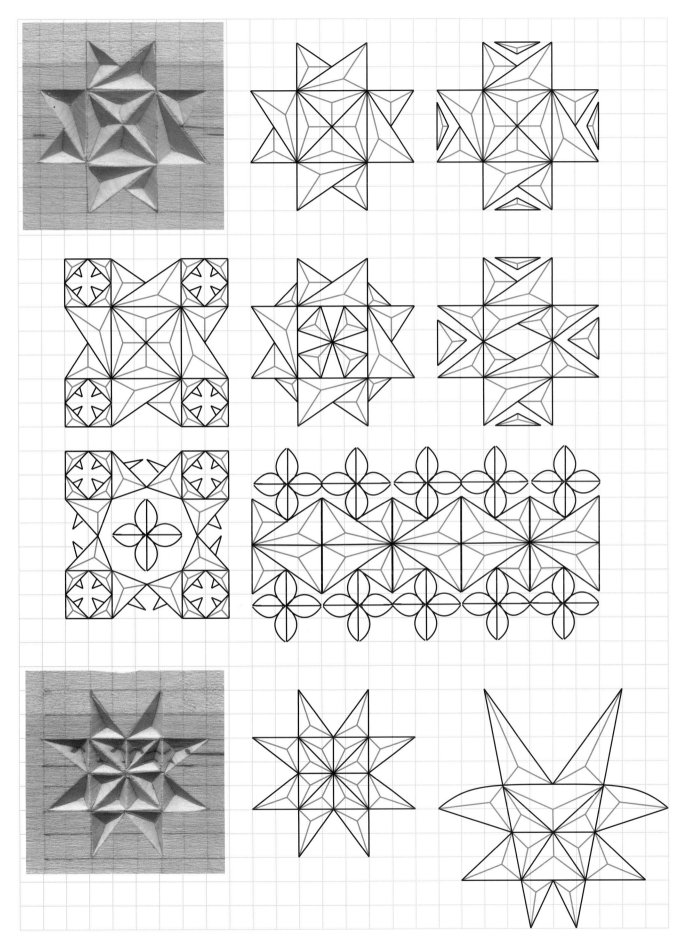

8 x 8 GRIDS

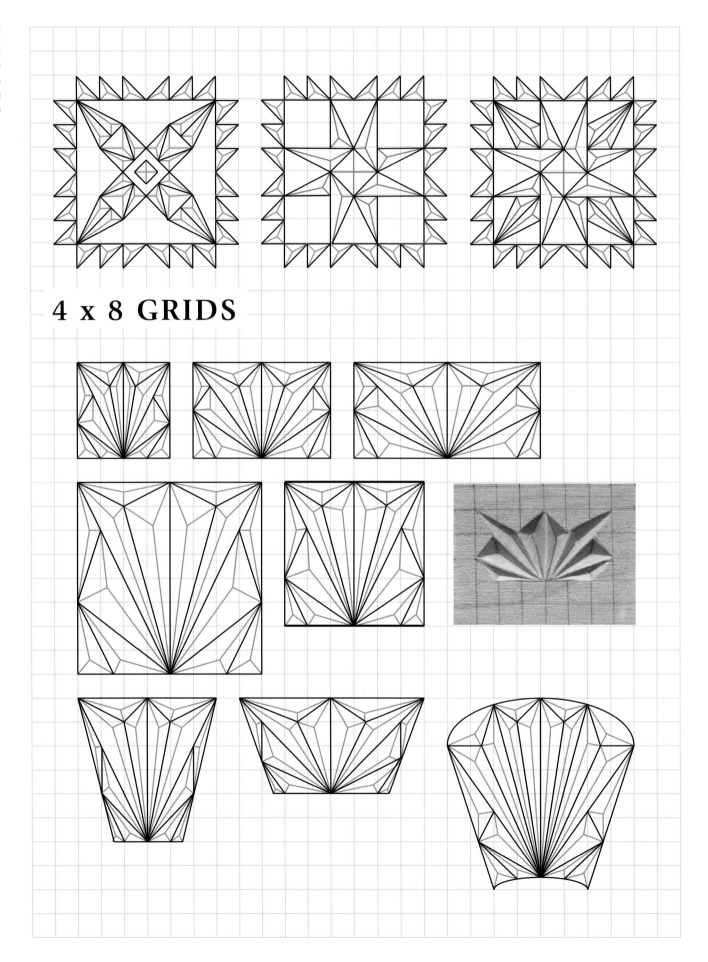

4 x 8 GRIDS

BORDER GRIDS

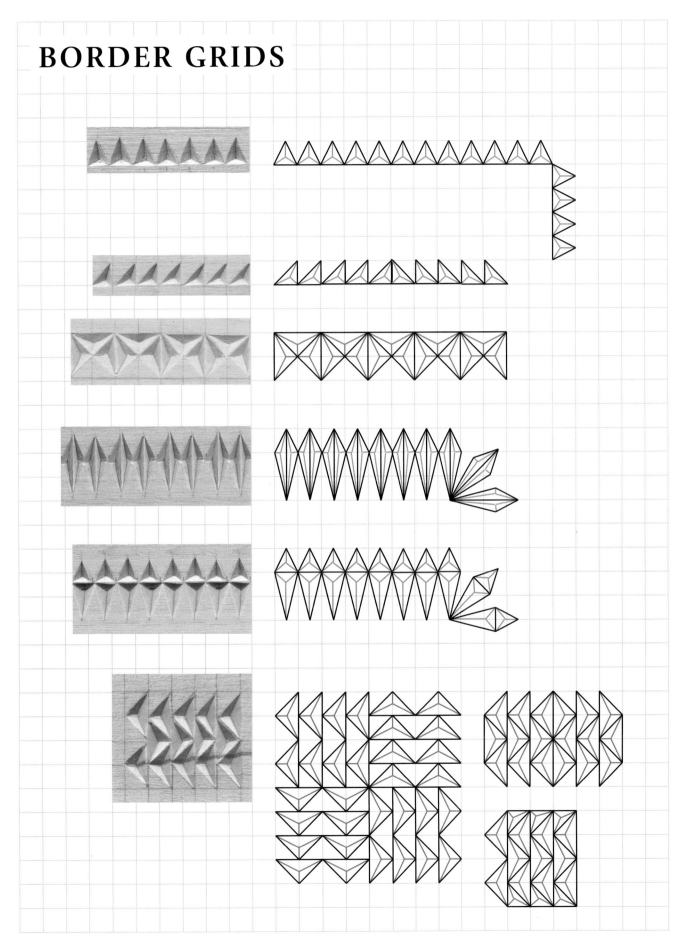

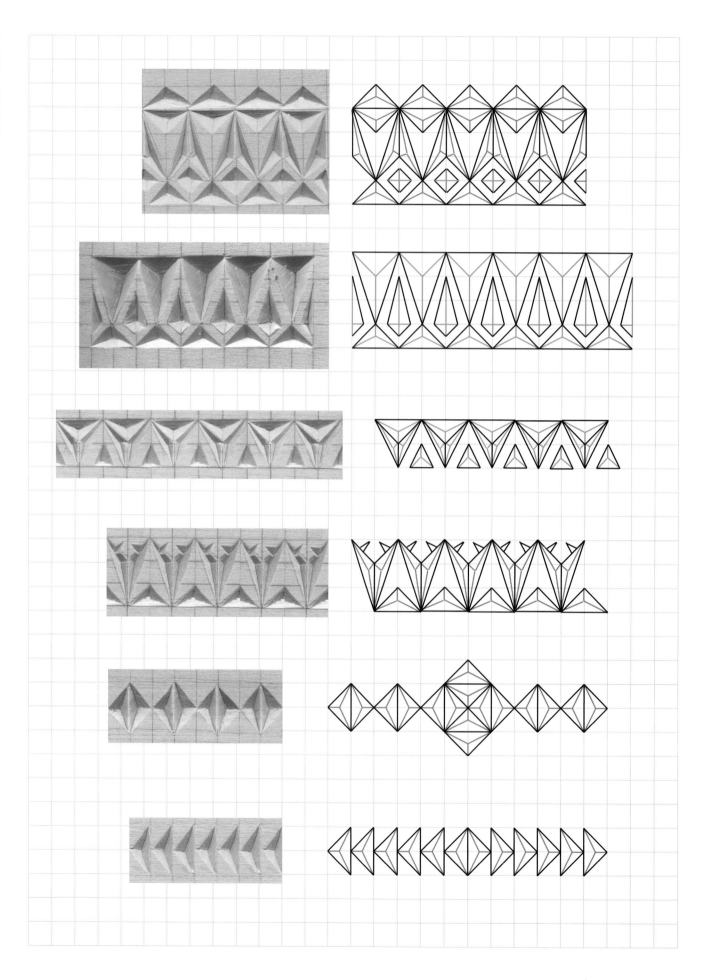

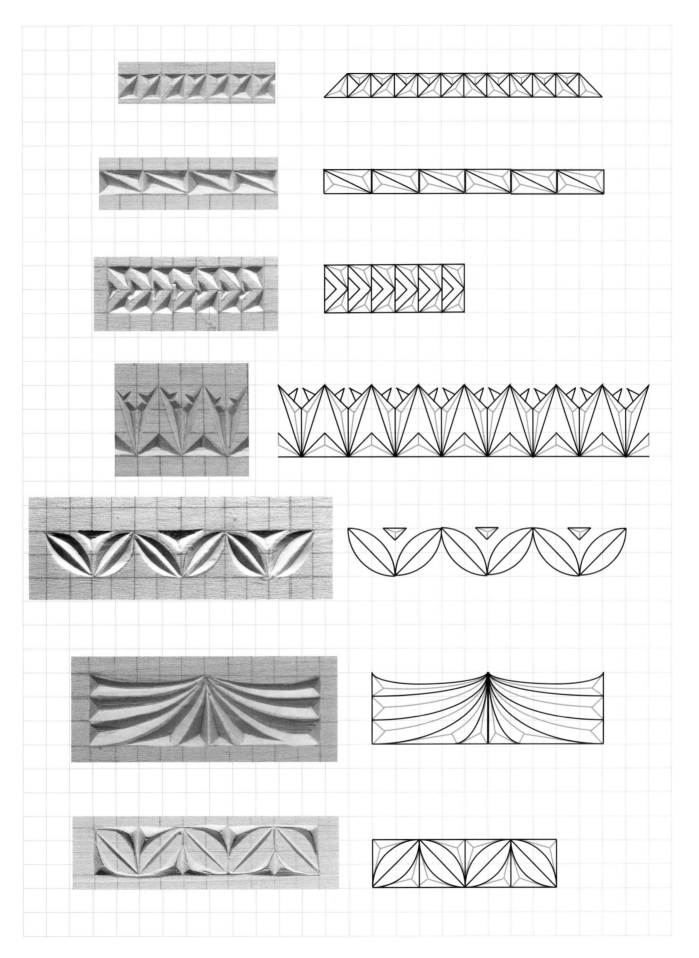

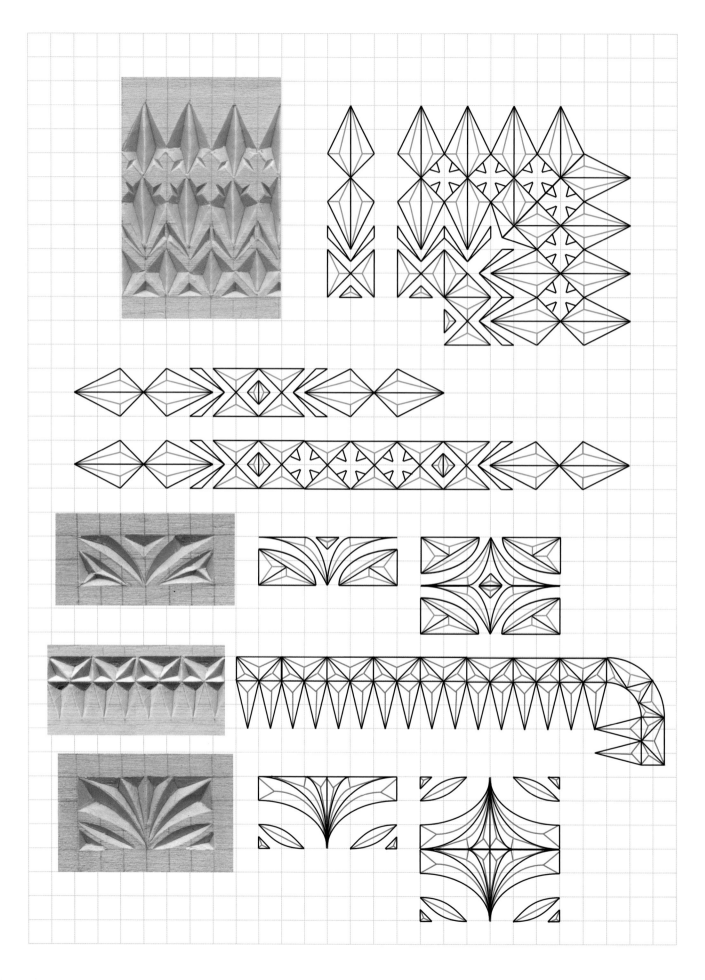

FILL PATTERNS

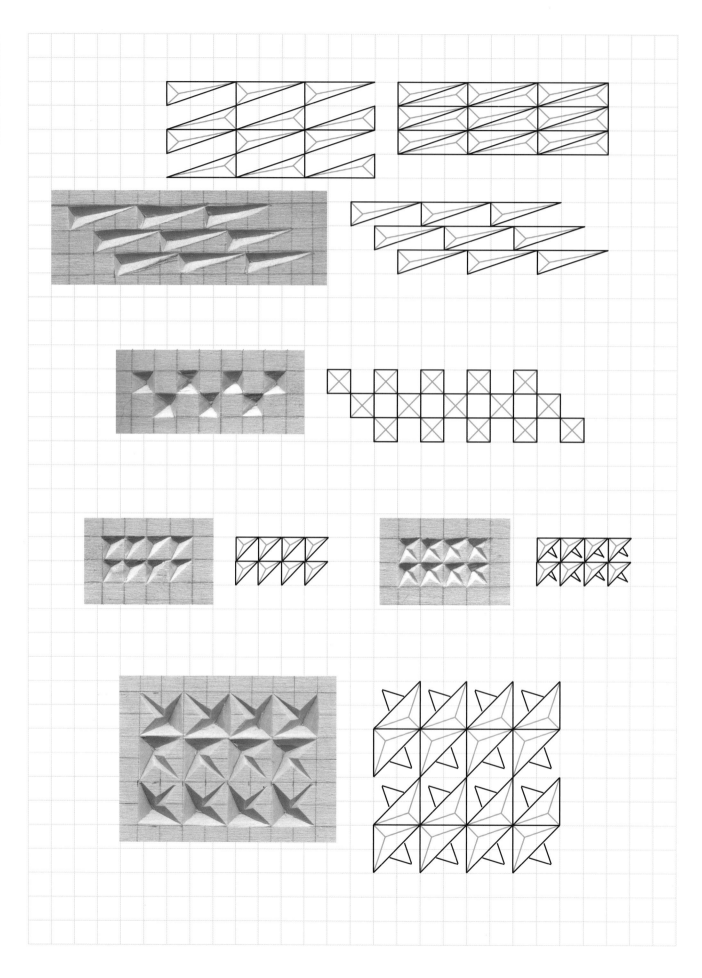

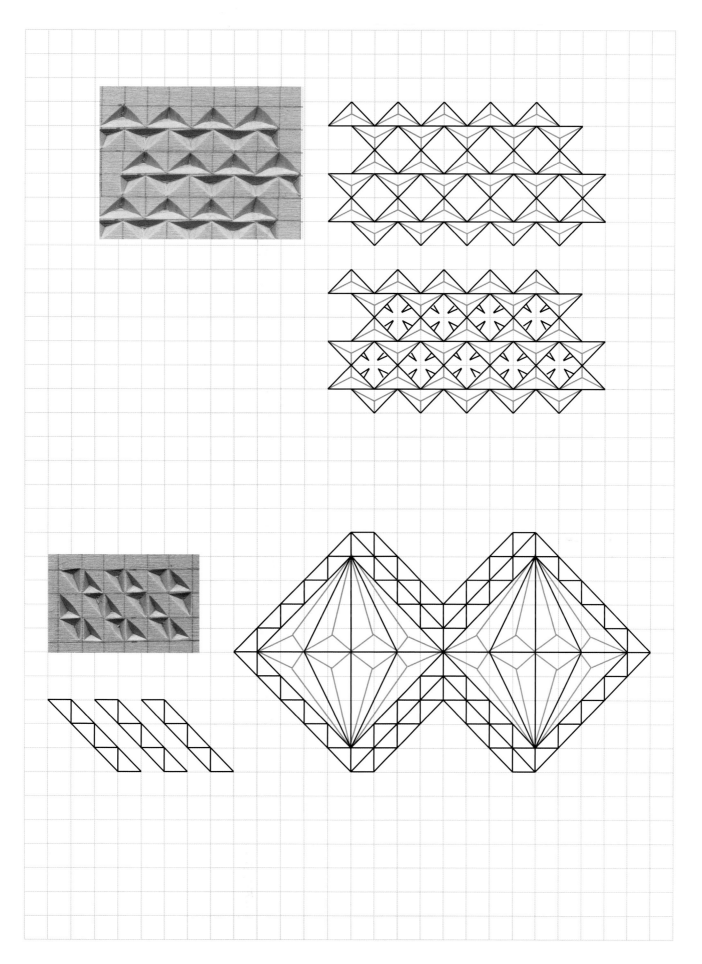

STRAIGHT WALL CUT GRIDS

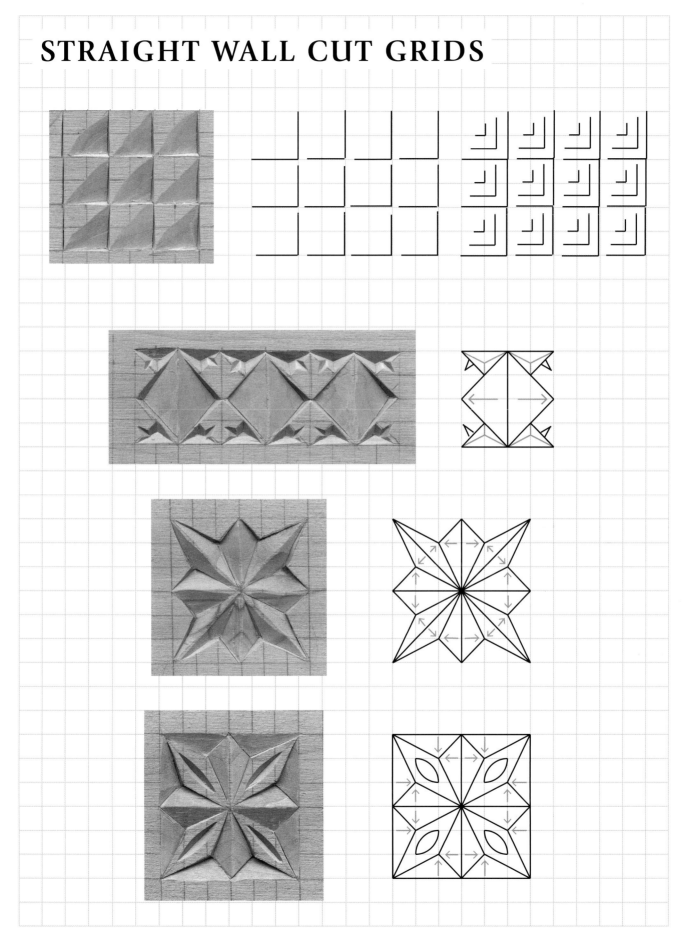

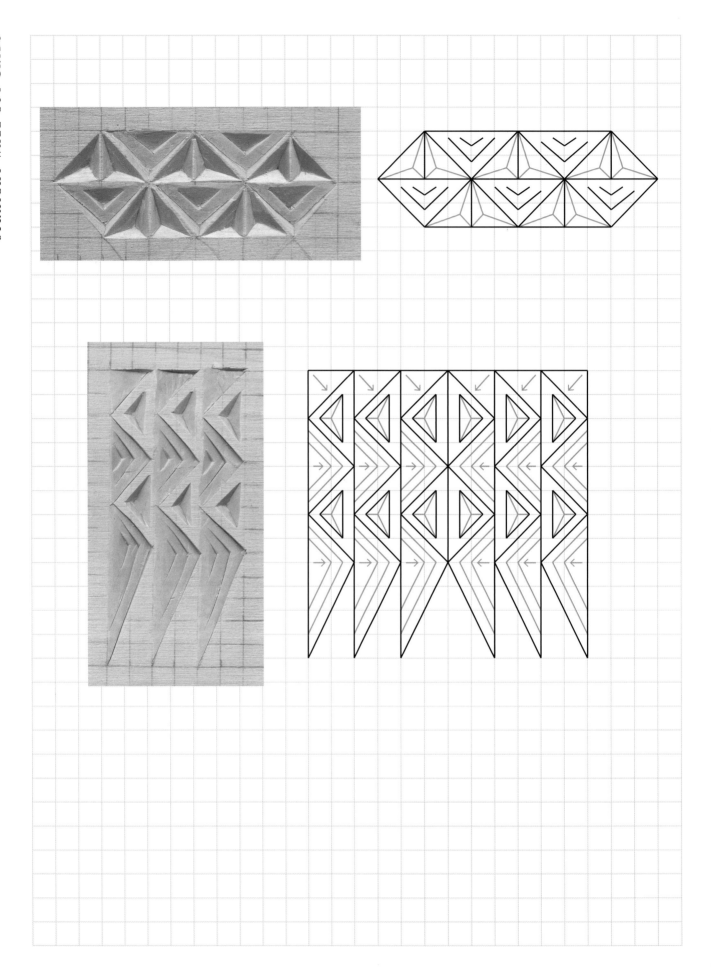

MISCELLANEOUS GRIDS

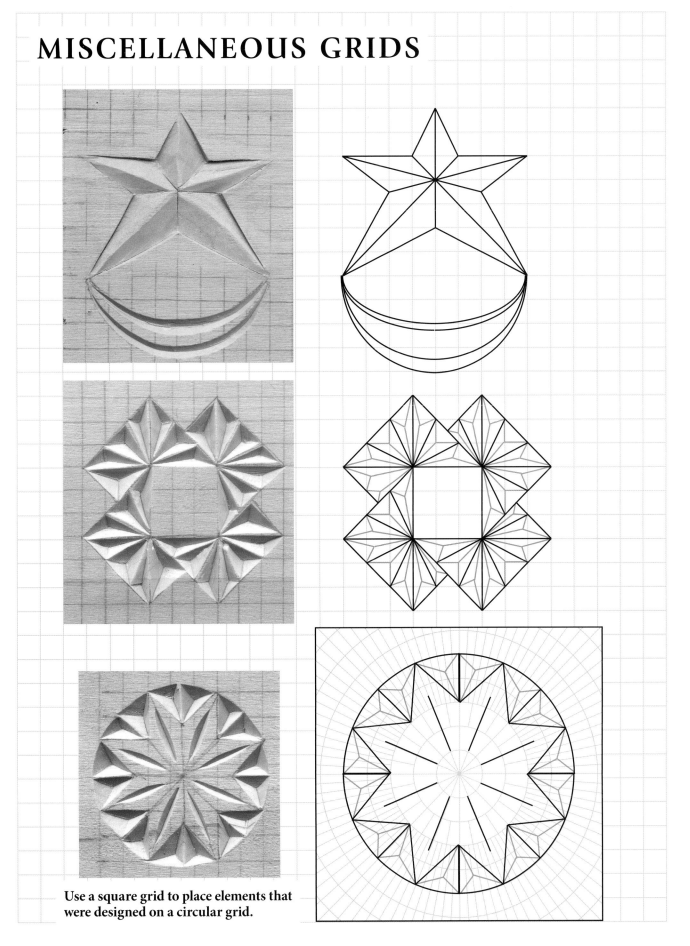

Use a square grid to place elements that were designed on a circular grid.

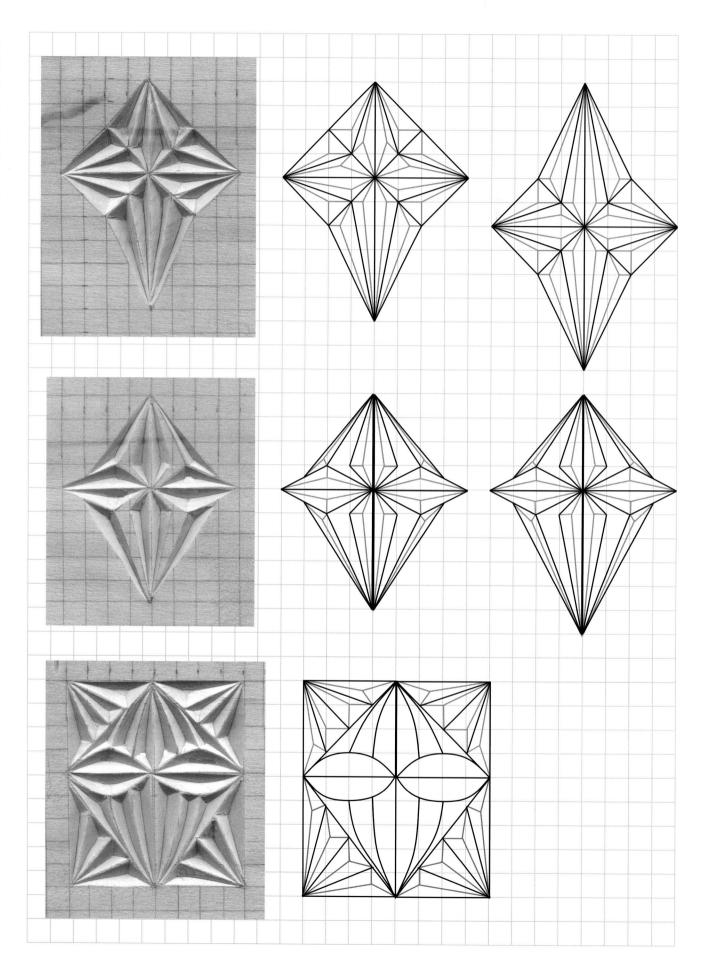

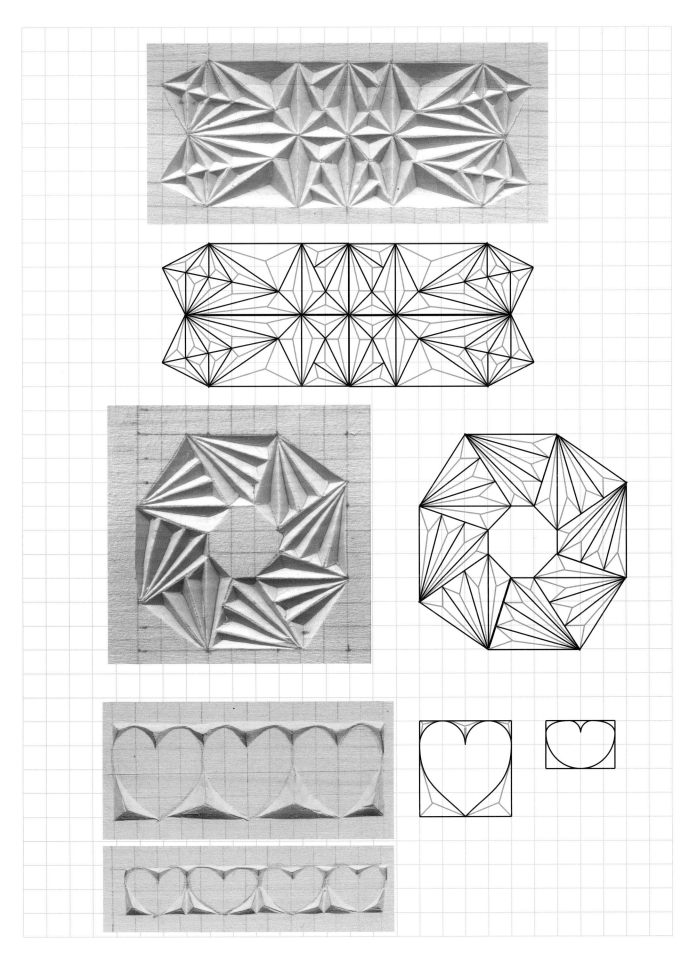

CIRCULAR LAYOUTS

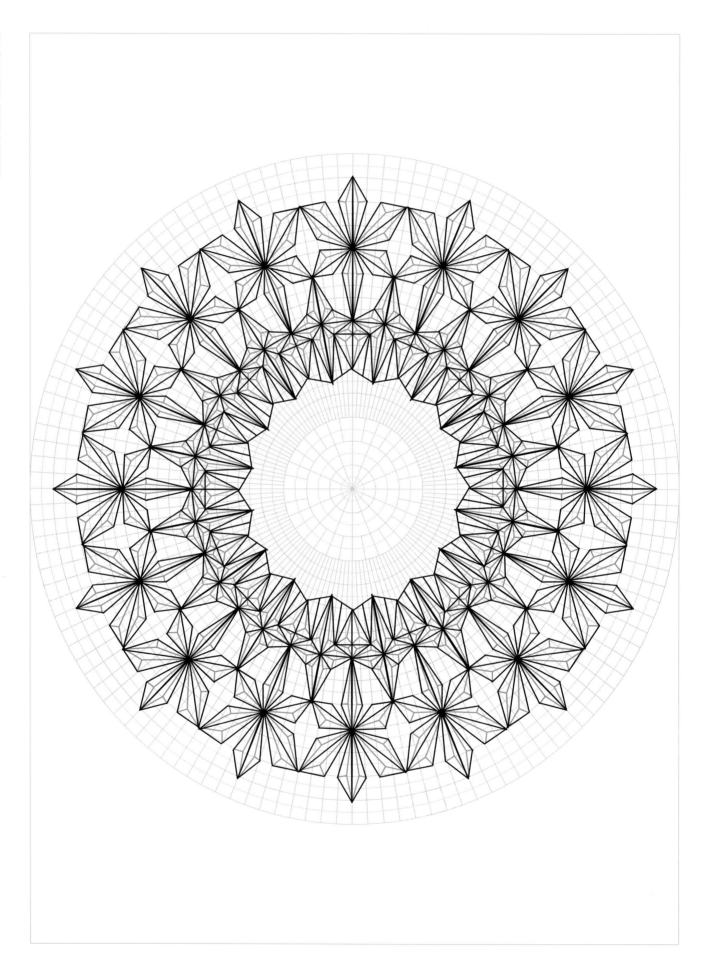

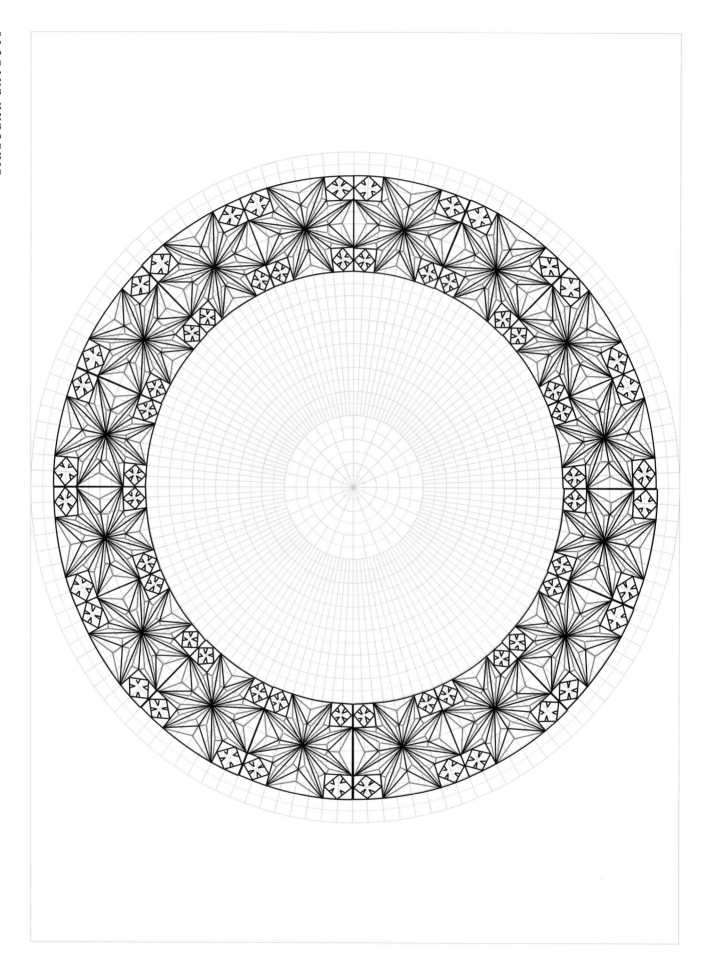

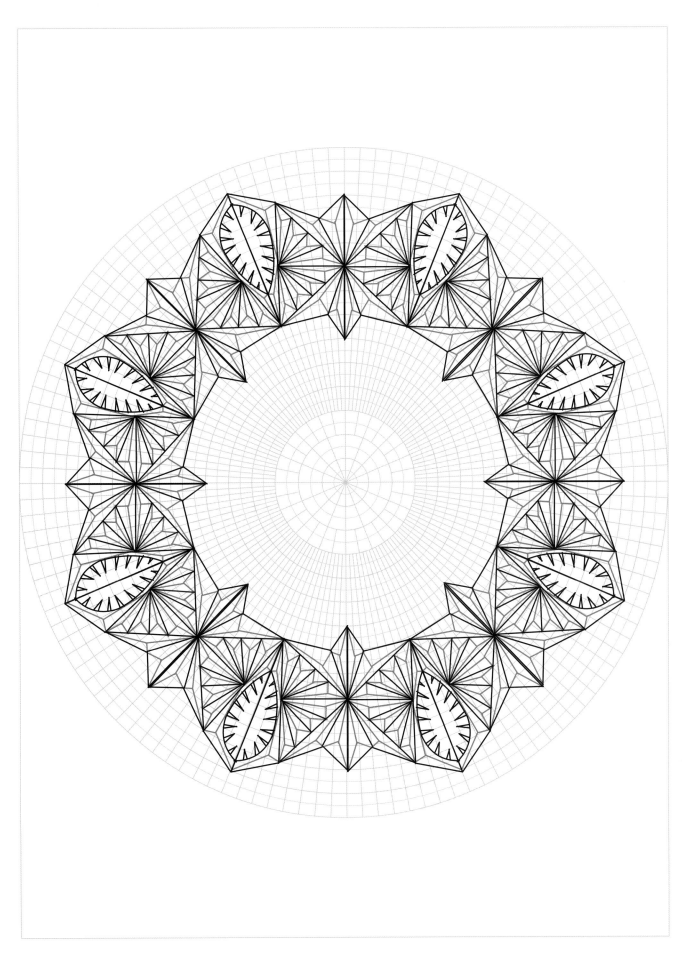

CENTERPIECE MOTIFS

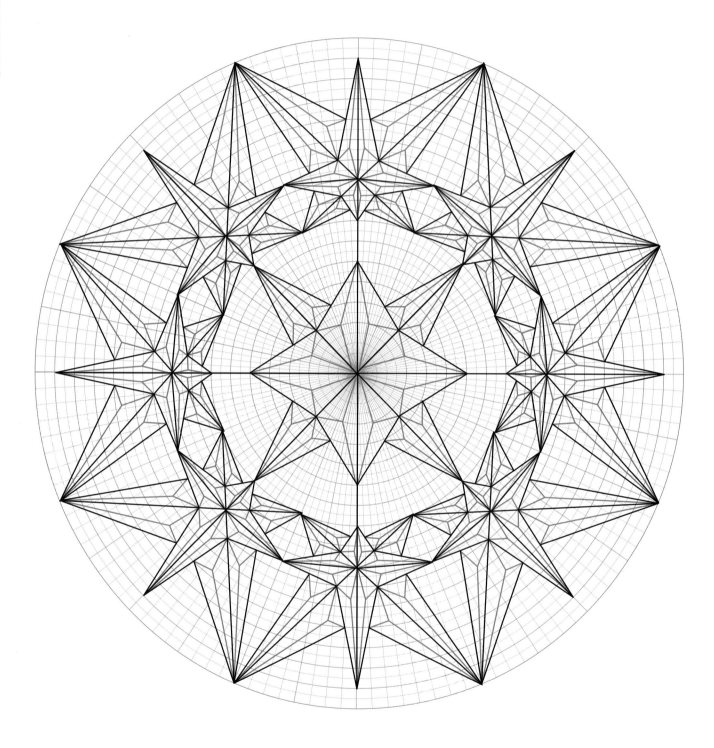

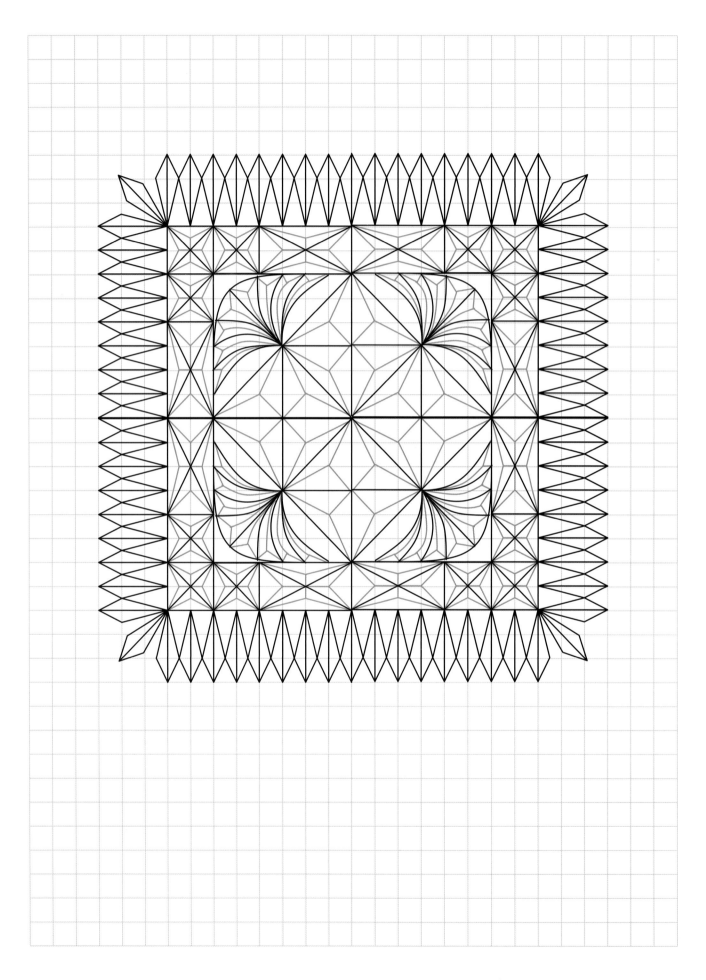

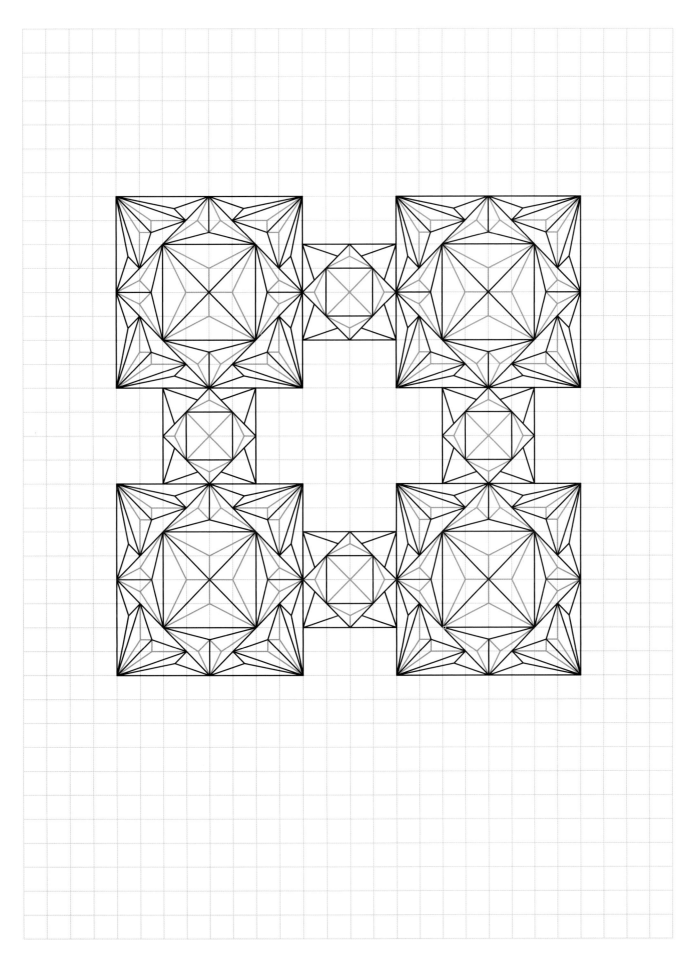

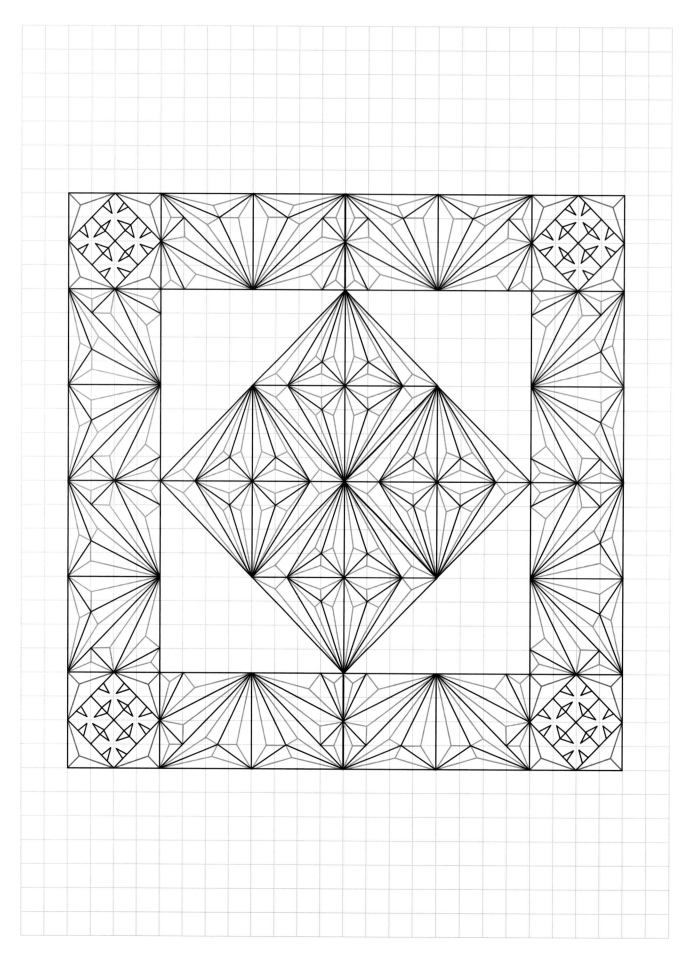

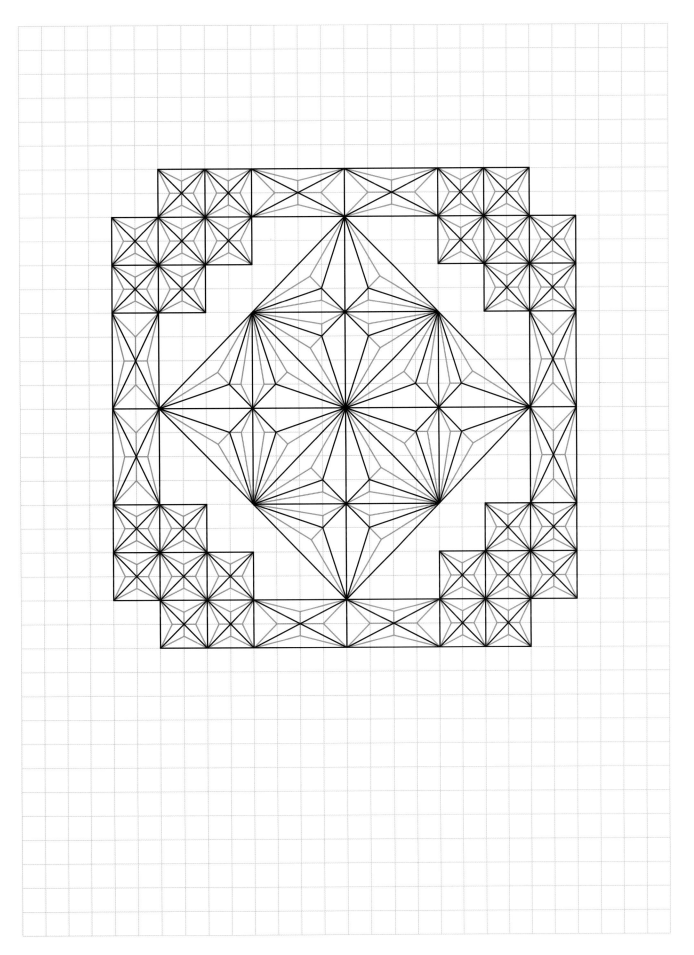

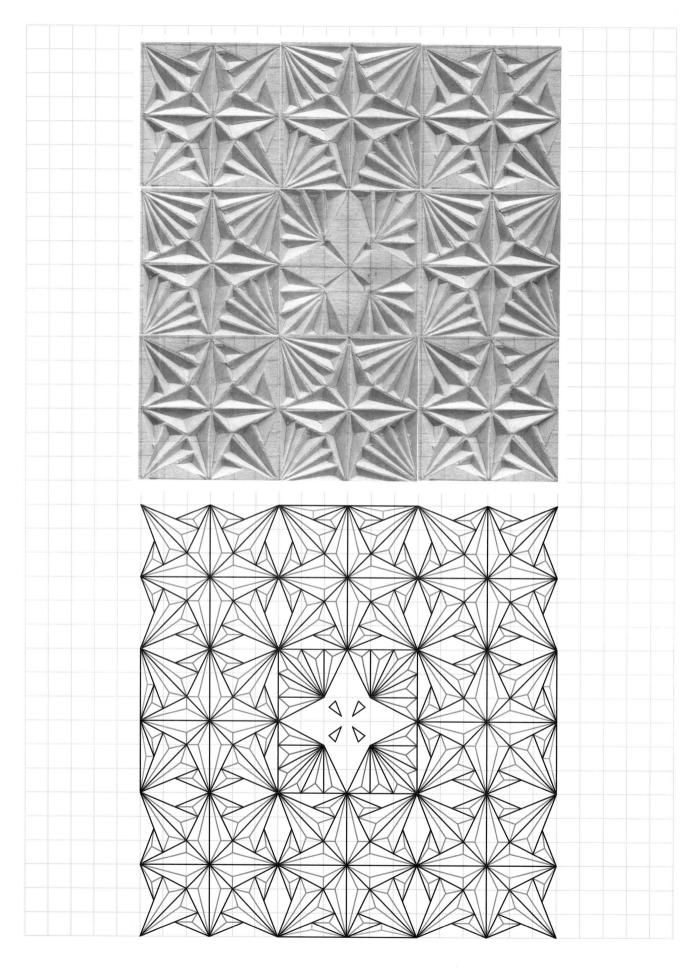

ORIGINAL PATTERNS

Heart Kitchen Trivet
Sized to fit Walnut Hollow 8" x 6" (205 x 150mm) oval plaque, #1836.

Free-Form Leaf Plaque

Enlarge pattern 140% to fit Walnut Hollow 12" x 9" (305 x 230mm) oval plaque, #1839. See photo on page 23.

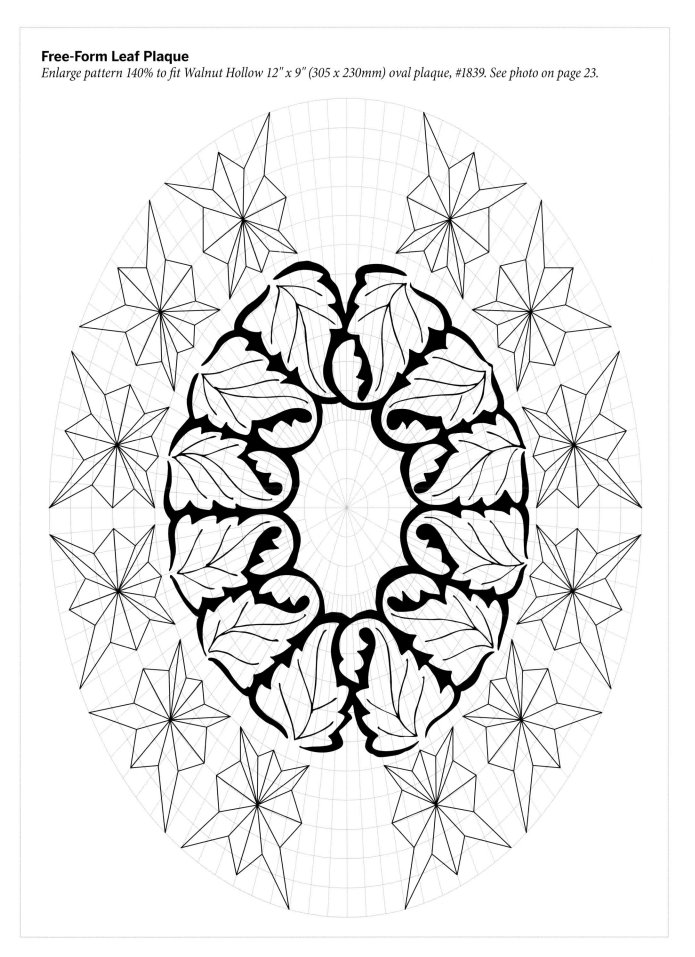

Large Candle Plate
See photo on page 4.

Small Heart Candle Plate

Sized to fit Walnut Hollow 9½" (240mm) Chippendale Plate, #3552. See photo on page 24.

Large Oval Kitchen Trivet
Enlarge pattern 140% to fit Walnut Hollow 12" x 9" (305 x 230mm) oval plaque, #1839. See photo on page 25.

Antique Wall Plate

Enlarge pattern 160% to fit Walnut Hollow 11" (280mm) Chippendale plate, #3553. See photo on page 24.

Fan Grid Candle Plate
Enlarge pattern 135% to fit Walnut Hollow 9½" (240mm) round plate, #3529. See photo on page 24.

Sample Grid Wall Clock
Sized to fit Walnut Hollow 14" x 11" (355 x 280mm) plaque, #18211. See photo on page 22.

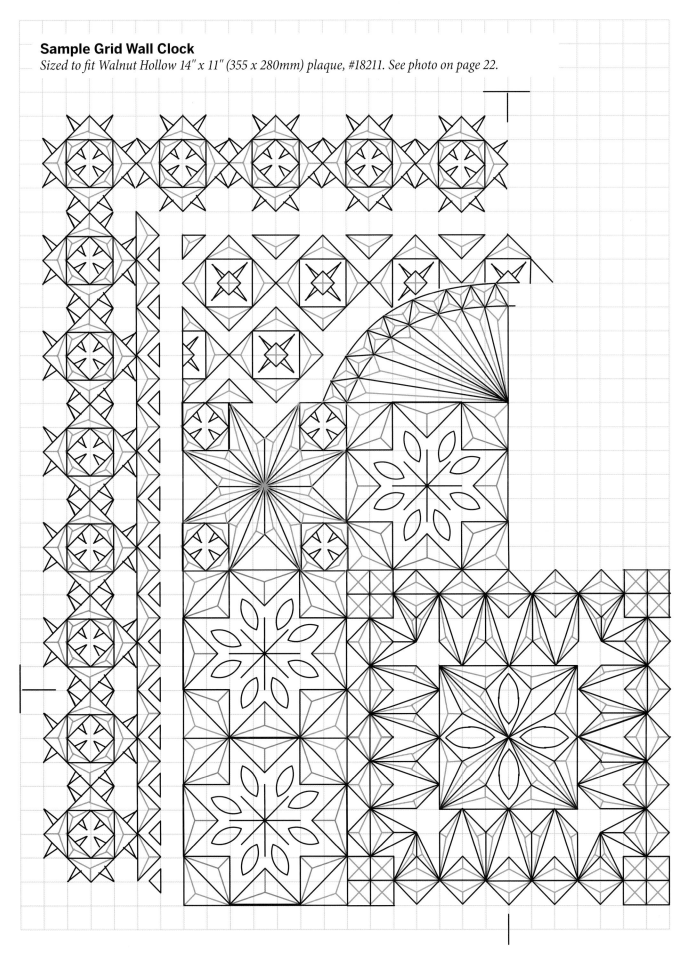

Individual Sample Grid Wall Clock elements

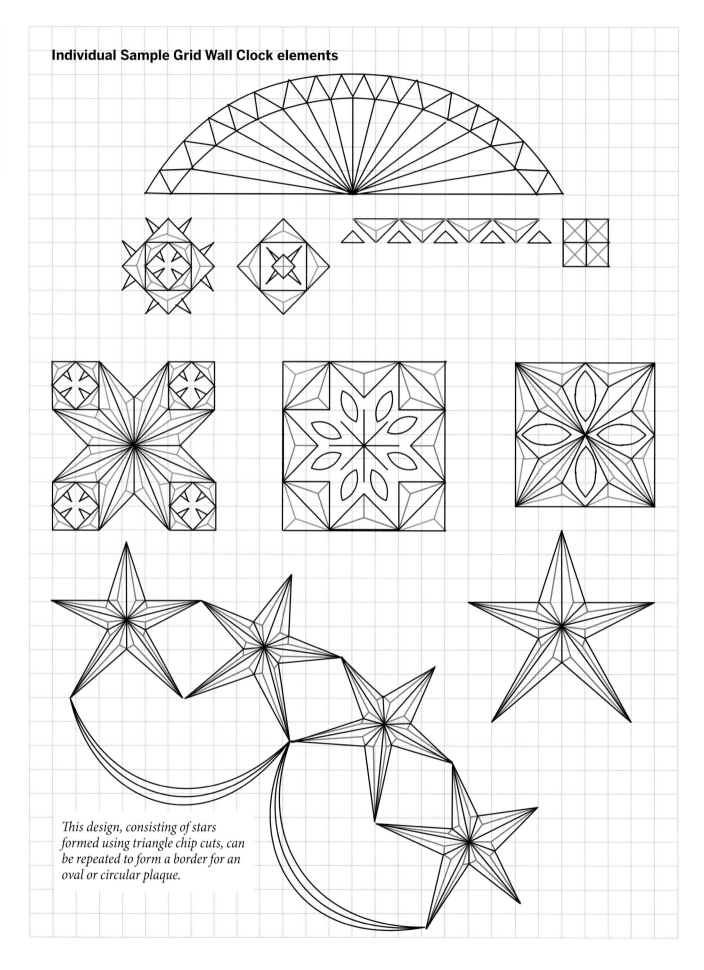

This design, consisting of stars formed using triangle chip cuts, can be repeated to form a border for an oval or circular plaque.

Oval Kitchen Trivet
Sized to fit Walnut Hollow 8" x 6" (205 x 150mm) oval plaque, #1836. See photo on page 23.

BLANK PRACTICE GRIDS

Sized to ¼" (5mm) squares, used for background to all charted grids.

Sized to fit 8" x 6" (205 x 150mm) oval plaque.

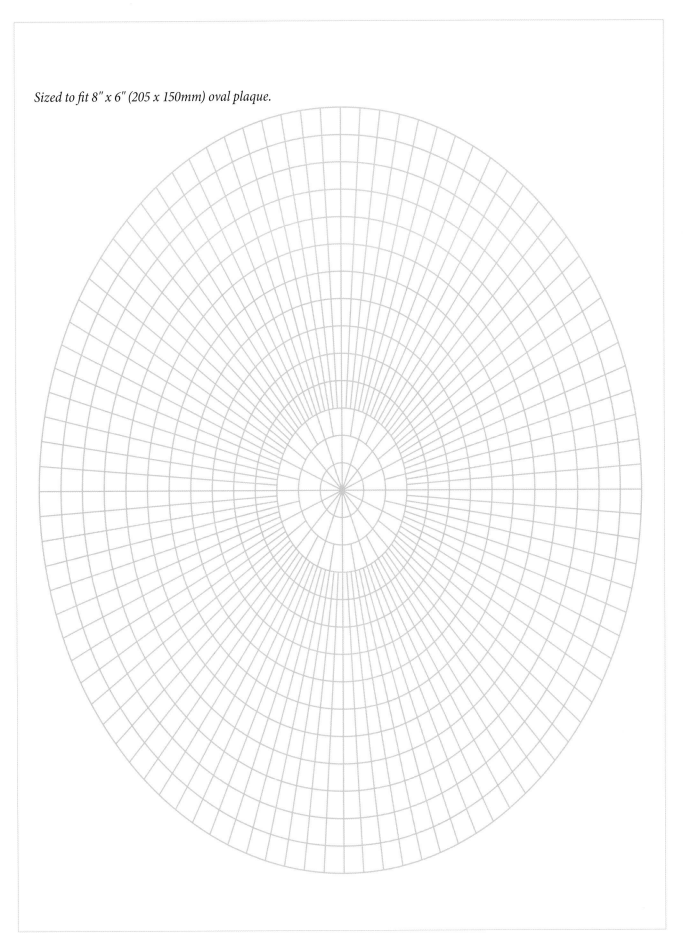

Can be resized to fit your carving blank.

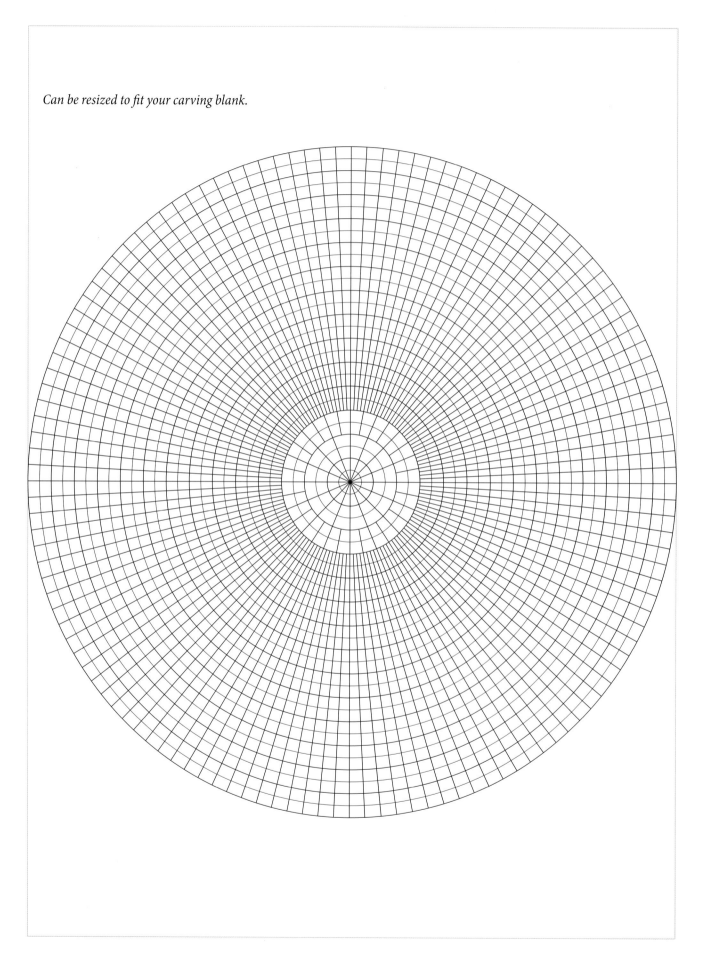

Index

Note: Page numbers in **bold** indicate gallery images.

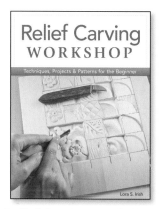

Relief Carving Workshop
ISBN 978-1-56523-736-0 **$19.99**

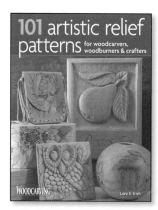

101 Artistic Relief Patterns for Woodcarvers, Woodburners & Crafters
ISBN 978-1-56523-399-7 **$19.95**

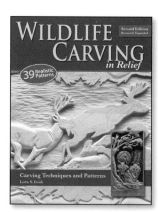

Wildlife Carving in Relief, Second Edition, Revised and Expanded
ISBN 978-1-56523-448-2 **$24.95**

Wood Spirits and Green Men
ISBN 978-1-56523-261-7 **$19.95**

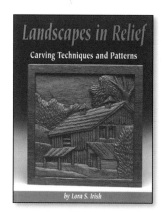

Landscapes in Relief
ISBN 978-1-56523-127-6 **$19.95**

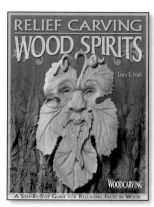

Relief Carving Wood Spirits
ISBN 978-1-56523-333-1 **$19.95**